Nationalism in the Nineties

D1382366

Nationalism in the Nineties

Edited by Tom Gallagher

Polygon
EDINBURGH

© Polygon 1991
22 George Square
Edinburgh

Set in Linotron Sabon by
Polyprint, Edinburgh and printed
and bound in Great Britain by
Redwood Press Limited, Melksham, Wiltshire

British Library Cataloguing in Publication Data
Nationalism in the Nineties
1. Nationalism
I. Gallagher, Tom 1954–
320.54

ISBN 0 7486 6098 4

Contents

Series Preface
CAIRNS CRAIG   vi

1. Introduction
   TOM GALLAGHER   1

2. The SNP Faces the 1990s
   TOM GALLAGHER   9

3. Nationalism, Journalism, and Cultural Politics
   CHRISTOPHER HARVIE   29

4. The Impact of 1979 on the SNP
   IAN O. BAYNE   46

5. The Lessons of Ireland for the SNP
   BOB PURDIE   66

6. The SNP and the Lure of Europe
   ISOBEL LINDSAY   84

7. The SNP and the Scottish Working Class
   TOM GALLAGHER   102

8. The Scottish Middle Class and the National Debate
   STEPHEN MAXWELL   126

9. Conclusion   152

10. References   159

11. Notes on Contributors   169

Series Preface

CAIRNS CRAIG

Scotland's history is often presented as punctuated by disasters which overwhelm the nation, break its continuity and produce a fragmented culture. Many felt that 1979 and the failure of the Devolution Referendum represented such a disaster: that the energetic culture of the 1960s and 1970s would wither into the silence of a political wasteland in which Scotland would be no more than a barely distinguishable province of the United Kingdom.

Instead, the 1980s proved to be one of the most productive and creative decades in Scotland this century — as though the energy that had failed to be harnessed by the politicians flowed into other channels. In literature, in thought, in history, creative and scholarly work went hand in hand to redraw the map of Scotland's past and realign the perspectives of its future.

In place of the few standard conceptions of Scotland's identity that had often been in the past the tokens of thought about the country's culture, a new and vigorous debate was opened up about the nature of Scottish experience, about the real social and economic structures of the nation, and about the ways in which the Scottish situation related to that of other similar cultures throughout the world.

It is from our determination to maintain a continuous forum for such debate that *Determinations* takes its title. The series will provide a context for sustained dialogue about culture and politics in Scotland, and about those international issues which directly affect Scottish experience.

Too often, in Scotland, a particular way of seeing our culture, of representing ourselves, has come to dominate our perceptions because it has gone unchallenged — worse, unexamined. The vitality of the culture should be measured by the intensity of debate which it generates rather than the security of ideas on which it rests, and should be measured by the extent to which creative, philosophical, theological, critical and political ideas confront each other.

If the determinations which shape our experience are to come from within rather than from without, they have to be explored and evaluated and acted upon. Each volume in this series will seek to be a contribution to that *self-determination*; and each volume, we trust, will require a response, contributing in turn to the on-going dynamic that is Scotland's culture.

1

Introduction

TOM GALLAGHER

The elevation of Alex Salmond to the leadership of the SNP in 1990 opened up a new phase in the history of the party. For the membership to opt for a leader who was only thirty-five and who had been briefly expelled from the party in 1982 for being part of a proscribed left-wing tendency, was an unusual fit of daring by a gathering which has usually preferred dependability over experimentation. Until 1990 the party had tended to mirror the behaviour of other Scottish institutions which have been notorious for driving some of our best talent overseas through their suspicion and neglect of creativity.

The cautious approach had its price, one that became increasingly steep as the party failed to intelligently exploit opportunities such as the imposition of the poll-tax and Labour's retreat from disarmament. The competent staidness which marked the leadership style of his predecessor, Gordon Wilson, belied the radicalism of the SNP's independence project and may have led to the party being overlooked by a section of the electorate willing to pursue radical solutions not stopping short of complete self-government. Salmond's energy, media skills, and the sharpness of his thinking means that the identity of the SNP is likely to be far less blurred in future. To a grassroots membership cheated of sustained electoral success, the prospect of dynamic leadership boosting the appeal of the party was enough to silence doubts about a responsibility so grave falling to one so young and, at times, impetuous. Winning the votes of 70% of conference delegates was a margin of victory that enabled the new leader to stamp his authority on the party.

Along the way Salmond outflanked the combined weight of the party traditionalists, that part of the left which identified with Jim Sillars, and the outgoing leader Gordon Wilson. Their criticisms centred around his relative youth and his lack of Westminster experience. These were strange reservations to emerge from a party keen to cut adrift from Westminster and supposedly contemptuous of the deference to age and experience which lay at the heart of the centralised political system. That such arguments were deployed suggests that the party remains very British in its instincts and behaviour despite the crusading rhetoric of its standard-bearers; if this is so, it means that one of Salmond's biggest tasks will be to infuse the party with the irreverence and unflappability which he has shown since his own arrival on the Westminster scene in 1987.

The membership did not just endorse Salmond on his own supposed merits as someone who represented the wave of the future. There was a high level of dissatisfaction against the hardline anti-Labour rhetoric of several prominent figures who lost out to supporters of the new leader in elections for key posts. Salmond's avowed strategy of pulling apart active Labour Party members from the leadership was preferred to blanket condemnation in the most scornful terms of all who were associated with the Labour Party. This was the tactic which had produced no electoral rewards and may only have encouraged the SNP's chief opponent to bury its own differences over contentious issues like Labour's defence policy and collection of the poll-tax.

The bulk of the SNP membership was unimpressed with the approach of Margaret Ewing, Salmond's rival for the leadership, which was to appeal to Scottishness across the political spectrum; internal differences were minimised, those responsible for Scotland's woes were excoriated, while a blueprint for turning around the situation to the Nationalist advantage was nowhere in sight. This idea of a seamless, sentimentally united Scotland had always appealed to those in the party who were oppositional by nature, or who had become content with belonging to a glorified national social club which indulged its Scottishness rather than a movement hungry for power. Despite the undoubted merits of Margaret Ewing, the fact that the strategy of continuity (or standing still) was rejected so comprehensively, may indicate a new maturity and sense of purpose among SNP activists.

This new mood is perhaps most evidence among younger members. They rallied behind Salmond, perhaps more than any identifiable group in the party, and provided some of his key campaigners. Salmond's appeal to them, based upon his relative youth and his refusal to disavow left-wing ideas, is obvious. The sense of confidence that he exuded was also appealing and may prove to be a vital factor in winning many converts from the 18-30 age group in the Scottish electorate. It has been described as the nationalist generation, one which because the chill winds of recession have blocked off emigration outlets elsewhere and because of a new-found belief in the worth of Scottish popular culture, is committed to Scotland and, therefore, is susceptible to a political appeal that can sketch out a realisable Scottish future rather than evoking a permanent sense of grievance.

Alex Salmond already has acquired a reputation for doing hard thinking about reshaping Scotland, which has appealed to younger members tired of sloganising and dogmatic postures. In 1989 he launched the *Scottish Centre for Economic and Social Research*, designed to be a clearing-house for new ideas and strategies. Membership is not confined to SNP card-holders but the aim of this think-tank is to give the party the intellectual clout which has rarely been its distinguishing feature. That activists see the link between clarity of thinking and electoral credibility was shown at the 1990 conference when well-known figures, who had been unable to complete policy documents on time, failed to be elected to senior party posts.

Salmond's own capacity for hard work lay behind his 1990 success as did his electoral track-record since being elected to parliament for Banff and Buchan in 1987. By 1989 the party was acquiring 53% of the vote in regional elections and what had been a Tory-SNP marginal looked like becoming a secure power-base for the SNP. Voters seemed prepared to judge Salmond on his ability to defend their interests rather than on the socialist label which his electoral opponents have been keen to draw attention to. Salmond's knack of devising a common message which transcends the urban-rural divide is one not much in evidence beforehand in the SNP. Perhaps it will enable the party to sound more convincing as it takes a stand on public issues, allowing it to dispense with the anodyne tones which in the past have betrayed the leadership's fear of alienating one of its specific constituencies.

Salmond is a lifetime member of the SNP who has never dallied with any other party. It is therefore all the more striking that he is the first SNP leader to admit publicly to being a socialist. However, he is probably on safer ground representing a seat in the North-East than in central Scotland. If Jim Sillars ever contemplated standing for the leadership, the need to devote round-the-clock attention to his seat in Labour's Clydeside heartland may well have dissuaded him. It is therefore strange that some of his supporters, in the bitterness of defeat, have complained about the party being under rural domination. The language of internal rivalry, whether it is based on geography, religion or social custom, inhibits Scottish self-confidence and it ought to have no place in the SNP.

The 1990s may be a time of opportunity for the SNP if the party starts to reappraise its role and questions methods of campaigning and organisation which have brought few rewards in a decade of long-distance right-wing rule that, from a distance, seemed to be tailor-made for a sustained SNP breakthrough. The party now talks about achieving independence by the year 2000 but nothing short of a relaunch may be necessary before that goal can be considered attainable. Even in the midst of grave challenges to the well-being of millions of citizens, such as the implementation of the poll-tax and the looming closure of Ravenscraig, into which the SNP has sunk much of its campaigning energy, the party can only make a fitful impact on the Scottish public. The marginal interest of electors in a party whose goal is to free them from their current discontents by restoring Scottish statehood, was shown by a polling survey which, at the end of the leadership contest, revealed that 40% of Scots did not know that for the past three months the SNP had been in the process of electing a new leader (another 24% of the sample was under the impression that Jim Sillars was the existing party leader).[1] Most people only give a moment's thought to the SNP during the shortlived weeks of a general election campaign. This is not surprising since the party is first, last, and always an electoral machine which ploughs its collective energies into an undertaking which an increasing number of electors do not think will make a blind bit of difference to their lives.

During 1990, the SNP was fixated first by the regional elections, then by its own leadership contest and finally, in November, by the two Paisley by-elections. Accordingly, it failed to get involved in the disputes surrounding Glasgow's year as 'Cultural Capital of Europe' which involved large numbers of concerned Glaswegians alarmed at the plans the city council had for transforming the face of the city, and the deals being struck with economic moguls to bring them to fruition. The sense of community possessed by many Glaswegians was under threat and it is surprising that SNP activists largely remained bystanders since political nationalism has so often sprung from a sense of community, especially where it is being undermined from within or without.

Glasgow's Labour administration (lulled by a runaway majority) left a number of hostages to fortune which the SNP was slow to exploit: an ambitious policy of economic reconstruction involving new retail and leisure industries that offer low-waged part-time jobs to a non-unionised workforce; efforts to dismantle the People's Palace, Glasgow's highly popular and successful social history museum seen as an obstacle in the way of redefining the image of the city; and, most audaciously of all, an attempt to sell off part of Glasgow Green to developers acting on behalf of the leisure and heritage industries.

A party with a keener awareness of how to grasp local political opportunities could have made much of what has turned out to be a Labour debacle by pointing out the way that people in the outlying peripheral housing schemes, where nearly one-third of Glaswegians live, have derived no benefit from the repackaging of the city, that indeed working people in these areas are effectively subsidising it in the form of low wages, high poll-taxes, and high rents. A party aware of how cultural concerns affect national consciousness would have made far more about the attempt to detach Glasgow from its Scottish surroundings, and package it for an international and Home Counties audience looking for spurious excitement by visiting a sanitised urban jungle populated by humorous and lively Glaswegians – real people of the kind that are increasingly thin on the ground in their worlds of marketing and high security, but ultimately reliable and unthreatening ones.

Blessed with a surer touch and a keener sense of how to operate when culture becomes politicised, the SNP might have exploited the unease sweeping the museums and libraries departments in the city as policies implemented from 'on high' place the needs of the leisure and heritage industries over the requirements of the ordinary users. Having successfully politicised national feeling, it is surely not beyond the party to do the same in the realm of culture, especially when the party includes talented artists and writers like Pat Kane and Colin Bell within its ranks.

Under Alex Salmond there is little danger that the SNP will stand still. It is likely to seek new, uncharted paths in an attempt to increase its relevance to the Scottish electorate, especially the young. There is no guarantee that it will meet with success which, in SNP terms, will remain measured by the inroads it can make into Labour's Central Scotland fiefdoms. The first major opportunity to advance in this direction under Salmond's convenership was provided by the twin Paisley by-elections on 29 November 1990. In both seats the SNP achieved a swing of around 12% which enabled it to rise from fourth to second place. The contest was another stage in the increasingly bitter civil war between two left-of-centre parties battling to claim ownership of Scotland's social democratic legacy. During the Thatcher years the 'bash the enemy' style of politics seemed the natural order of things. However, her relish for confrontation and for sowing divisions within her own party proved too much, first for the electorate and eventually for those MPs who sustained her in office. Her removal in the midst of the Paisley by-elections spoiled a good old Scottish punch-up in that burgh but it remains to be seen whether the major contestants have taken on board any lessons from her demise.

Thatcher's attempted revolution from above failed because the conflict she generated within her own party and throughout society destroyed the cohesion necessary for a new political consensus, replacing the one discredited in the 1970s, to take shape. Scotland is not so different from England for entrenched political division not to have similar results. After all, political activists inside and outside the SNP working to make Scotland a self-governing entity have been engaged in just as bold an undertaking as Mrs Thatcher when she sought to roll back the state and turn politics into a process for forging a society based on free market principles. Their task has been to break down the voting public's low self-esteem and instinctive dependence on London-based policies by forging a belief in Scottish capacity to devise its own agenda and take increasing responsibility for its own affairs. However, the infighting over tactics and the distribution of electoral rewards is likely to subvert people's faith in the Scottish constitutional revolution in just the same way as many who first voted for Thatcher in 1979 concluded that the political price of her revolution, based on unchecked individualism, was too steep to pay. It remains to be seen whether Alex Salmond feels a complete rethink in strategy is in order for the 1990s; or whether he thinks that a refinement of the go-it-alone approach, in which the SNP presents itself as the only force that can rescue the Scottish people from its long-term misfortunes, is still the right strategy. If so, the mind-set that prompted the party to shun the Constitutional Convention will prevail, along with language used by Ian Lawson at the Paisley South election count when he rounded on Labour hecklers with the cry, 'We're going to get you. You're played out.'

Salmond may feel that to let up on Labour as a general election looms closer is plainly unrealistic. But the level of aggression the SNP directs at its chief foe is in danger of discrediting politics as a worthwhile activity from which citizens can expect a better future. Outside the small and shrinking band of political activists in Scotland, the rage and hatred which are the trademarks of those competing for the urban, lower-income vote in Scotland produce bewilderment and distaste. Alex Salmond hopes that in the event of a fourth Labour defeat or a weak Labour government that fails to dent the legacy of the Thatcher years, party activists committed to Home Rule will cross over to the SNP irrespective of the abuse they have received hitherto. However, it is more likely that they will stay where they are or channel their energies away from politics. The aggressive tactics of the SNP may unwittingly have reinforced the existing party boundaries in Scotland during a period when they ought to have been more flexible. The emphasis on depicting the party as the agent of salvation rather than seizing the opportunities for confidence-building contained in a citizens-based movement like the Constitutional Convention, shows the SNP to be peculiarly British in its political orientation. The lessons of eastern Europe, where people-based movements shook the status quo, have been lost on the bulk of the party leadership. The Convention could have created a uniquely Scottish agenda that might have decoupled a large section of the electorate from Westminster. As it is, the British political scene continues to exercise domination in Scotland despite the self-examination of the Thatcher years. People know only too well that their life chances and immediate prospects are determined more often than not in the English South: if Labour elects a new leader from the ranks of its Scottish MPs, or if a less regionalist Tory government decides to redistribute a little of the wealth of the South-East by switching significant numbers of government jobs to Scotland, then Westminster will be demonstrating its power of initiative to recast the Scottish dimension of politics almost without the blinking of an eye.

The conditions of the 1980s bred a sense of national self-assertion, whose roots may prove shallow in the world of post-Thatcher politics. Bold anti-system parties which adhere to fundamentalist positions often repel electors once they glimpse the fact that ideological purity comes before their own interests. The German Greens found themselves relegated to the margins of politics in 1990 after such a voter backlash. A short time before, their standing among German youth was even higher than that of the SNP among Scotland's youthful voters, but their introspection and dogmatism has enabled the Social Democrats to recapture the youth vote. The SNP may be faced with a similar eclipse if it proves unable to bring the emotional needs of the party into alignment with the target voter's desire for a less confrontational form of politics. No seat currently held by the party is safe and it remains to be seen whether the communication skills of the new leader will boost the appeal of the party outside territory favourable to it, or merely disguise structural shortcomings that weaken the party's standing. The party's electoral fortunes are usually decided by events beyond its control and a world overshadowed by the threat of chemical and trade wars as the 1990s get underway may yield up electoral advantages as well as drawbacks.

Whether or not the changes at the top in the SNP are matched by a shift in its electoral fortunes, this is certainly an appropriate moment to examine the party's relationship with key social groups in Scotland, its relationship with other interests that are shaping national consciousness, and its role in the debate concerning the future of Europe and Scotland's place in it.

The essays here advance thoughtful and often provocative points of view and the volume is marked by its diversity of opinion and the strength of its argumentative content. It is offered as a contribution to the debate on Scotland's political future in a decade which will see fresh opportunities to break old political moulds but where the capacity to exploit them may still prove to be as elusive as before.

2

The SNP Faces the 1990s

TOM GALLAGHER

A quarter of a century has elapsed since the Scottish National Party first began to win elections. In the preceding three decades since its emergence in 1934, the stability of the British two-party system had dashed all hopes of making inroads among the Scottish electorate. The SNP's first breakthrough occurred in a 1967 by-election when Winifred Ewing, a Glasgow lawyer, stormed the Labour citadel of Hamilton in industrial Lanarkshire. Only in retrospect is it clear that the timing of the win was far more significant than its location. Back in 1945 Dr Robert McIntyre had actually held the nearby seat of Motherwell for the SNP after a by-election win as a result of disregarding the wartime electoral truce observed by the major parties. Motherwell was promptly lost six weeks later in the 1945 general election as Hamilton would be in 1970. At the end of 1973 the deprived inner-city seat of Glasgow Govan was captured by Margo McDonald whose impressive media performances caused many Scots, for years afterwards, to assume that she was the leader of the SNP, but it was a seat she could only hold for three months until another general election intervened.

Each success in the urban industrial belt has proved an unreliable indicator of the SNP's future prospects. It has always performed least consistently well in the very area of the country where it needs to make a strong showing if its goals are to be realised.

Hamilton occurred as the Wilson government was entering a trough of unpopularity, unprecedented for any post-war government. The threadbare nature of its plans to modernise and reform an underperforming economy and an antiquated political system had been quickly exposed in Wilson's second term. Labour lost badly in 1970, its reputation having been permanently damaged by the opportunism and evasion that marked its six years in office. The Heath government's equally ambitious programme centred on leading an economically competitive Britain into the EC was derailed by serious industrial unrest and the explosion in world oil prices.

At the nadir of the Heath government's fortunes in 1973-4, the SNP experienced a second breakthrough. Not only was Govan captured but in the two general elections of February and October 1974, the party caused a sensation by winning seven seats and 22% of the votes in the first, and eleven seats and 30% of the votes in the second contest. To jubilant Nationalists and indeed to many fearful members of the established parties, it looked as if the political map of Scotland was being permanently transformed and that a new power in the land was stepping forward. But experience has shown that it is only in very unusual circumstances (for instance such as those in Ireland after 1916) that a new untested force like the SNP can engineer such a fundamental change in mood, especially given the nature of the British electoral system.

Between 1966 and 1974 a large part of the UK electorate's faith in the established party system and its ability to manage the country was being undermined but not to the point of serious political instability. Third parties were able to absorb the votes of many of the discontented in 1974, as they turned away from two discredited parties led by relatively unpopular individuals. This trend got underway in Scotland earlier than in the rest of the UK as a result of the vulnerable manufacturing sector experiencing the first chilling effects of a failing economic strategy after the mid-sixties. The SNP thus saw their advance in terms of specific Scottish happenings rather than in the wider UK context. This is perhaps excusable since the hasty decision of the minority Labour government to offer Scotland a devolved assembly of its own (for which little genuine enthusiasm existed at senior party levels) indicated that senior figures regarded the 1974 Scottish results as being much more than a local extension of those in England – where it had been the Liberals who had been the beneficiaries of unprecedented third party support *at exactly the same moment as the SNP*.

In its 1973 report, the Kilbrandon Commission, set up to review the workings of the British Constitution, had discerned the role of the SNP to be that of a barometer of discontent rather than a mass movement inexorably leading the country towards some form of self-government:

> The greatest significance of the Scottish national movement lies not in its advocacy of separatism but in the means which it has provided for the people of Scotland to register their feelings of national identity and political importance.[1]

Ian O. Bayne, a longstanding member of the SNP and contributor to this volume, has elaborated elsewhere on the reasons for his party's 1974 breakthrough in terms that complement Kilbrandon's viewpoint:

> At the two 1974 elections the SNP clearly benefited considerably from the phenomenon of 'tactical voting' – and nationally, at least as much from ex-Tory voters voting to 'keep Labour out' as from ex-Labour voters voting to keep out the Tories. At the same time it is perfectly possible to argue that the party also attracted – from all sides of the political spectrum – a proportion of genuinely radical 'floating voters' who were quite simply disenchanted with the traditional 'two-party system' and with the kind of 'adversary' and 'class war' politics that it typified and who saw in the SNP an increasingly credible 'third force' alternative of precisely the same sort as the SDP is now apparently capable of offering the people of England.[2]

The concluding sentence betrays the face that the letter was written in 1981 as the newly created Social Democratic Party (SDP) was benefiting from a fresh bout of voter-alienation from the two major parties. 1981 was a year in which government-inspired deflationary policies produced a massive downturn in manufacturing productivity, resulting in a wave of company bankruptcies and record post-war unemployment, a traditional manufacturing sector like Scotland being particularly badly hit; it was a year which presented the spectre of the Labour opposition locked in a factional struggle that threatened the survival of the party and was to repel voters in their millions.

These were conditions that might have seemed ripe for further SNP advance. But the party had been hopelessly stalled ever since the devolution project, which Labour had dangled before it, floundered in 1979 due to an insufficiently high turnout in the referendum required by parliament, which had inserted the pre-condition that the backing of at least 40% of the entire electorate was needed before a Scottish Assembly could be ratified.

A rueful Jim Sillars, reflecting in the mid-1980s, identified serious flaws in the thinking of proponents of self-government in the 1974-9 period:

> We failed completely to take account of the nature of . . . the two great parties of the English state, Labour and Tory, the power of the Whitehall departments and the deep reserves of experience these institutions had accumulated over many years in dealing with awkward problems that came from unexpected angles . . . I didn't probe. Nor did anyone else. At a time when we should all have been engaged in acute thinking and analysis, we enjoyed the emotional ride instead. At home the Assembly was taken for granted. . . . Had we all been prudent, the

Establishment would not have been successful in pushing us in their desired direction . . . which was to wear us down by attrition and win by chicanery.[3]

On the self-government question the Labour government had seized the initiative from the SNP, which did not have the political skills or experience to win it back – or to distance itself from the Labour Party when the 1978-9 'winter of discontent' destroyed its authority and turned the 1 March 1979 referendum into a verdict on the recent performance of the incumbent government rather than a springboard for an assembly in Edinburgh. Associated by necessity with a floundering government on which Scotland's hopes for self-government, however modest, depended, the SNP was unable to offer itself as a fresh alternative in the 1979 election. The Home Rule cause had been tarnished by the failure of a government whose demise brought the curtain down on post-war consensus politics. The right-wing economic liberalism of Margaret Thatcher cut little ice in Scotland as shown by the defeat of Teddy Taylor, her chief Scottish standard-bearer, but the Tories were able to recover enough votes to dislodge the SNP from most of the seats captured in 1974.

In a state of shock, the party withdrew into itself and engaged in a brief but damaging bout of infighting between radicals, who felt that the key to the future was to make an explicit socialist appeal to win over recalcitrant Labour voters and gradualists who favoured a broader centrist message. It was very much a Scottish variant of the feud taking place in Labour ranks and a telling indication of how the SNP is prone to unconsciously imitate wider trends in British politics. To its credit the party patched up its differences more smoothly than Labour did (or the two centre parties were destined to do upon merging in 1988) but its relevance, even as a protest vehicle, diminished in 1983 when it was a distant fourth behind the Liberal-SDP Alliance, and in 1987 when it achieved a net gain of one seat but lost Gordon Wilson who had held the party's only urban Scottish constituency (Dundee East).

In a November 1988 by-election those who had written off the SNP as a spent force were confounded when Jim Sillars, its best-known figure, captured the Labour stronghold of Glasgow Govan. He was the beneficiary of a mood of discontent with Labour which, in 1987, had received its best-ever Scottish results, but thereafter had proved unable to defend ordinary supporters threatened by deeply regressive Tory measures in education, social welfare, housing and, above all, local government finance thanks to the introduction of the poll-tax in Scotland one year ahead of the rest of the UK.

A lot of working-class Scots felt abandoned in the face of this Tory juggernaut, with Labour's prospects of regaining office slim. But, by the time of another by-election in the neighbouring seat of Glasgow Central, only seven months after Govan, the mood had changed. Opinion polls started to reveal that Labour might just be electable in the English South where discontent with the effects of government economic policy was mounting. Disaffected Scots proved less amenable to the Nationalist message and endorsed Labour at the by-election and at the European elections held on the same day when all but one of Scotland's eight seats were taken by Labour. Once again here was an election that revealed how possibly the bulk of Scots were still influenced by events and trends in the rest of the UK when making key political choices.

Such had been the case even when the SNP had been the beneficiary of significant voter support in the late 1960s and 1974. Scotland may have possessed a distinctive four-party system by the 1990s with the largest party in England facing the threat of total eclipse north of the border, but major party upsets had occurred at similar moments in the electoral cycle elsewhere in the UK for the same overriding reason – dissatisfaction with the performance of central government or else with the failure of the chief opposition party to offer a credible alternative. The SNP had still to break out of the cycle where it occasionally found itself acting as the magnet for large numbers of protest votes.

It is unfortunate for the SNP that what electoral success it has enjoyed, has come in short, often unforeseen, bursts rather than incrementally over a longer period of time. Instead of producing a measured outlook, such an experience tends to distort perspectives and encourages the party to opt for a series of short-term, often high-risk, strategies like that in the run-up to the various elections in 1989 and 1990, when so much was staked on discrediting Labour's record over the poll-tax and offering in its place a high-profile SNP-led campaign of resistance. When such a strategy fails to deliver an electoral reward, it is often difficult to avoid internal strains and recriminations.

Perhaps the SNP would be wrong-footed less often if it was to realise the conditional nature of its support and devise strategies to invoke a more enduring appeal, one possibly not based around elections. It is understandable that such enlightenment failed to dawn in the 1970s; success came quickly, too quickly as some party members acknowledge in retrospect. The SNP did not have time to sink deep enough roots in the body politic. Loyalty to Britain was disturbed but never broken. The Scots saw the party as a useful tool, for securing reform and expressing grievances (as the party acknowledged in its own literature). Few Scots accepted the claim that they were so different from their English neighbours as to make separatism a necessity, or that central government was to be equated with oppressive English government. In the 1980s such perceptions enjoyed wider currency, thanks to the partisan loyalty the Thatcher government could generate among key social groups in the South and its attempt to use Scotland as a testing-bed for policies which Scottish electors had repudiated in successive elections – but in the absence of much confidence in the ability of any locally based party to do much about it.

In the 1980s, faith in politics as a worthwhile vocation or as an agent of social improvement has slumped as the declining membership of all of Scotland's political parties makes clear. The infighting and self-serving party propaganda that emanated from the non-Tory camp which was quick to proclaim Scotland's opposition to Thatcherism but careful to avoid finding common ground that could turn such opposition into more than rhetoric, was an unedifying spectacle and a recipe for further depoliticisation.

Briefly at Govan, it looked as if the SNP was capable of pursuing a different approach in which it did not see its political opponents as enemies to be destroyed, and was mindful of the need to restore a sense of civic responsibility to people by repudiating the tradition of UK adversary politics and developing an enabling patriotism with like-minded people in other parties. But the new agenda which might have enabled the SNP to sink deeper roots in Scottish society was not pursued. The party was carried away by the Govan result and, unmindful of the ephemeral nature of past electoral upswings, viewed it as an endorsement for its latest strategy of 'Independence in Europe'.

This policy rested on the premise that, like other small nations, Scotland could play a full role in the European Community that would guarantee it a viable future as a self-governing unit and would nullify the danger of 'go-it-alone' separatism frequently raised by opponents, as well as the handicap of being part of a centralised state in which it was largely excluded from major decision-making. It was undeniably an attractive and thought-provoking policy which allowed the SNP to depict itself as in the mainstream of European developments, unlike the Prime Minister whose October 1988 Bruges speech revealed implacable hostility to European political integration, however long the timetable. Although local conditions and the calibre of the candidate were more instrumental than the 'Independence in Europe' flagship in determining the outcome of the Govan by-election, the SNP's opponents were placed on the defensive by the appeal of the slogan. Donald Dewar, Scotland's chief Labour spokesman, even came out in favour of 'Independence in Britain' in a panicky effort to steal the SNP's thunder.

The test-run of 'Independence in Europe' was to be in the June 1989 European Elections. Accordingly, partisan feelings mounted in the wake of one by-election triumph and in anticipation of further advances in an even more crucial contest. Nationalist enthusiasm for cross-party initiatives was therefore lukewarm just at a time when one that had been long in the making finally reached fruition. This was the Constitutional Convention which, in 1989, began its task of drawing up a scheme for a Scottish parliament or assembly. It was the brainchild of the Campaign for a Scottish Assembly and the credibility of the proposal mounted as patient lobbying won the backing of a swathe of influential bodies and individuals in Scotland that helped to shape public opinion. Shortly before the Govan by-election, the Labour Party gave its backing to the scheme after much prevarication but, ten weeks later, the SNP pulled out, unimpressed by the concessions made towards its own conditions for entry centring around representation on the Convention, a commitment to the sovereignty of the Scottish people, and a multi-option referendum including the option of 'Independence in Europe'. Space does not exist to fully unravel the complex negotiations that preceded the first meeting of the Convention on 30 March 1989, but several observations deserve to be made.[4]

A more alert and sophisticated SNP might have grasped the enormous significance of the Labour Party associating itself with an essentially nationalist project. The party had long hesitated about whether to get so entangled with the Convention exactly because it was far removed from its normal role of representing a class interest in politics. It meant treating SNP politicians, once branded as opportunists or cranks, as partners in a common endeavour and giving them the opportunity to go before the Scottish public as mature, responsible individuals able to operate on the inside track of Scottish politics rather than be perpetual outsiders continually protesting about 'the game being rigged'. Labour's preparedness to enter the Convention at a time when the SNP was in the ascendancy did not stem from altruism but arose from the failure of their strategy to rely on gradualist change emanating from Westminster to satisfy Scottish grievances. It was a strategy producing rising frustrations within a party which had even spawned an articulate self-government wing.

A less embattled nationalist party might have regarded these developments as a tribute to its patient advocacy of a Scottish dimension in politics and obtained quiet satisfaction from the 'tartanisation of the Labour Party'.[5] However, the majority view, as articulated by Jim Sillars, was that 'the Labour Party was going to use the Convention to make mincemeat of a numerically weak

SNP'.[6] Surveying the party's 1989 retreat into fundamentalism, an SNP advocate of cross-party dialogue sadly observed that:

> ... a breakthrough will result not on the basis of our class appeal but our Scottish appeal. We are never going to win by playing the game on Labour's territory; the trick is to make them play it on our territory which is precisely what was beginning to happen in the Constitutional Convention, a fact which makes the party's withdrawal from it all the more incomprehensible.[7]

In a democracy, a party that prefers isolation and begins to exhibit growing concern for ideological purity and unwillingness to compromise, is displaying the classic characteristics of a party in decline. It is too early to suggest that the SNP is facing such a prospect but it is not without significance that its high polling scores evaporated after the Convention withdrawal, returning it to its pre-Govan norm by the end of 1989, with no further victories having been achieved in that year.

Near the close of 1989, Jim Sillars expressed puzzlement at the way 'folk agree with every word we say and then vote Labour'.[8] This conundrum may have something to do with the fact that it is often a party's presentational approach rather than the content of its policies which makes the most impact on voters. A party with a greater sense of Scottish history ought to have been aware of the debilitating effect of rancorous feuding between parties or religious interests (of the very type that has marked the SNP-Labour relationship of late) on Scottish self-confidence. Thatcher and her circle are totally unhistorical in their bid to change the character and direction of English life: it is what makes them so bold and reckless. If the SNP peered into the national past, some might be surprised at the parallels with the present and at how internal strife has increased the domination of a powerful neighbour.

Irate nationalists might respond that they need look no further back than the 1970s to gain the historical insight necessary to determine their strategy towards Labour and a cross-party initiative such as the Convention. Not without a great deal of cause, the SNP feels that it was double-crossed by a party that briefly stole its nationalist clothes on espousing devolution and then was able to avoid the electoral retribution for the failure of devolution which instead was bequeathed to the hapless SNP.

1979 had a profound impact on the SNP which haunted it through the 1980s. In personal terms it was akin to a great personal shock which robbed the sufferer of self-confidence and the ability to view his situation with a clear perspective. Ian O. Bayne, a party member of nearly twenty-five years standing who has not aligned with any particular faction, has been a regular contributor to debates about the party's strategy; he is therefore well equipped to examine how the party has attempted to cope in the 1980s with the daunting legacy of the failed deliverance of the 1970s still dogging its path, as he does in his chapter on the impact of the 1979 referendum on the party.

1979 had the kind of effect on the SNP equivalent to the way that the soaring hopes of Irish nationalism in the early 1920s were dashed by a messy compromise which inexperienced negotiators in London signed with devious opponents, leading to civil war and the destruction of a united nationalist movement. Scottish Nationalists have been heard to say that the tangled Irish experience is scarcely relevant to Scotland but, as Bob Purdie shows in his chapter on the Irish connection, this is not so and, sooner or later, the party may find itself going through the process that led Irish negotiators to London at the end of 1921. The separatist wing of the Irish nationalist movement has never, to this day, recovered from the way its hopes were relegated by that document: the compromise has coloured its attitude to politics and to co-operating with other political forces ever since.

It would be tragic if a fixation with 1979 was to have such a mesmerising effect on the SNP, causing it to judge the behaviour of present-day actors against what happened during a decade which will soon belong to a past century. That would be a case of being trapped by history rather than learning from it. To believe that Labour remains the same old predatory unionist beast that sold Scotland short with a booby-trapped form of devolution in the 1970s is an exercise in self-delusion that damages nationalist credibility. Closet unionists and reluctant home rulers continue to populate the Labour Party, but there is abundant evidence that they are outnumbered by members at all levels who desire reinforced self-government of a kind that cannot be clawed back by any Westminster government.

For many of the Labour home rulers, 1979 and the way that Scottish wishes were disdainfully ignored by the most centralist government seen in the lifetime of voters, had as profound an impact as the events leading up to the election of Thatcher had on the SNP. Self-government moved on from being a legislative afterthought to appease or dish the Nationalists to become a central requirement. Many Labour activists, and not a few vocal MPs, now put their passion for self-government ahead of their desire to exercise power in London. SNPers should regard this as a tribute to the way that they have moved the Scottish question from the 'lunatic fringe' of politics to centre-stage. For Jim Sillars and senior colleagues to disregard the changes of the 1980s and to insist that 'Labour is unionist to the core' is ultimately self-defeating. It probably reinforces the influence of closet unionists who seek to use blanket SNP hostility to close ranks against any concessions to 'neo-nationalism' as happened to some extent in 1990. It has not so far impressed those advocates of independence who, in opinion surveys, reveal themselves to be Labour voters with no intention of switching. The SNP will wish to corral their votes since a failure to encompass the entire independence-minded electorate weakens the credibility of the party. But the SNP needs to realise that individuals in politics can still perform high service for the cause of self-government without being members of their party.

The lack of strategic insight may stem from the failure of the party to sink deep enough roots in Scottish society. No institution, no region of the country, no section of society has been clearly won over to their cause. Traditionally, the SNP has drawn its support more evenly across the spectrum than any of its competitors.

Significantly, it has never won majority support from any cohesive middle-class interest, even though its leadership is mainly drawn from the professional middle classes. In 1979 the middle class was the section of Scottish society least enthusiastic about devolution with only 35% of AB voters intending to vote 'Yes'. Stephen Maxwell has set himself the task of identifying why the Scottish middle class failed to seize the opportunity of Scotland's new wealth in the 1970s to secure a major adjustment of the economic balance in favour of Scotland; why those in the public sector evinced so little ambition for the public welfare of Scotland, for the extension and improvement of the services they provided for the people of Scotland, or even for their own and their children's career prospects in Scotland. He points to the limited opportunities to exercise public leadership in Scotland which was a consequence of the post-war expansion of the existing public sector and the nationalisation of private concerns brought under the control of distant Whitehall. He thinks it conceivable that the large-scale recruitment of non-Scots in the Scottish public sector has hindered the growth of 'a critical mass' of Scottish consciousness and ambition. But it is in the cultural not the political sphere that the incapacity of the Scottish middle-class is perhaps most clearly revealed. Maxwell reckons that 'it is the lack of vitality of the middle-class Scottish imagination that brings us closest to the mystery of the Scottish middle class'. There is a striking dearth of imaginative literature about the character and experience of the Scottish middle class which points to a remarkable absence of self-awareness – 'the inarticulate Scot is revealed as typically middle-class not working-class'.

But a rudderless middle class has not fallen in behind the Thatcherite project and indeed has shown great obstinacy in resisting it. This may be because (as Tom Nairn has cogently argued elsewhere) the Scots have an historic corporate identity more invested in public sector institutions such as the kirk, the law, and education than is the case in any other part of the United Kingdom. Having been heavily involved in the institutions of an expanding British state and empire up to 1945, the expanding public institutions of the post-war consensus were a suitable replacement for those of contracting overseas colonialism.[9] The arena of public corporatism could hardly be expected to create a dynamic or radical middle class prepared to take a leap into the dark. But resistance to the application of market prescriptions to their respective occupational sectors or professional concerns has created an oppositional middle class. However, constitutional reform does not qualify as a unifying theme. The absence of informal structures of civic and intellectual dissent of the type that emerged in eastern Europe is one clue as to why not. Despite the impetus Thatcherite shock-treatment has given to grassroots campaigning, most notably over the poll tax, Scottish political opposition remains heavily institutionalised in large organisations like the Labour Party, COSLA, and major trade unions which have a powerful vested interest in controlling and limiting the growth of dissent.

According to Maxwell, there are grounds for believing that the middle-class will adopt a more radical stance in the 1990s. The old corporate order in Scotland has been weakened so that a greater scope exists for middle-class mobilisation outside vested political interests. The impact of environmental issues and the European factor are undermining conventional perspectives, the diversification of the Scottish media, and the growth of Scottish 'think-tanks' with varying degrees of independence from political sponsors, holding out the prospect of the Scottish middle class playing a weightier role in the Scottish debate.

The role of the middle-class in determining Scotland's future assumes increasing significance because of the numerical decline of the formerly much larger working class. Between 1974 and 1985 Scotland lost one in three of its manufacturing labour force. However, the concentration of the working-class in towns and cities along Scotland's lowland corridor, and a pattern of voting that has grown steadily more uniform since the 1960s, has turned it into a seemingly secure power-base for the Labour Party. Such is the reliability of its core lower-income following that, in certain parts of Scotland, notably Glasgow, it is the middle-class which has been the most obvious beneficiary of the politics of urban regeneration. So commanding was Labour's position after 1987 that it found itself not just the dominant party among the Scottish working class but among the Scottish middle-class as well. Since the shift of middle-class allegiance is a very recent and perhaps only temporary phenomenon, and middle-class interests are adept at getting politicians to safeguard their interests, Labour's concern for this important new constituency is hardly surprising.

But on past form it is surprising that, since 1979, no backlash has occurred among working-class voters upon finding that Labour is unable to defend their living standards against attack. The results of the May 1990 regional elections showed that the cost for Labour local authorities of implementing the poll-tax was a very meagre one. Even prominent poll-tax rebel Dick Douglas MP was unable to weaken the grip of the Labour establishment when (following his resignation of the Labour whip and expulsion from the party) he stood in a Fife regional ward on the basis of his unconditional opposition to the poll-tax. Admittedly, it is somewhat unusual for a sitting MP to contest a local election, but it is instructive to compare his fate with the leader of the Oxford Tory councillors who resigned their seats over the poll-tax around the same time: he was re-elected while Douglas seems in danger of disappearing into oblivion having failed, at least on this occasion, to enlist working-class backing for his 'no poll-tax' challenge.

The failure of the SNP to capitalise on its vigorously fought non-payment campaign in the 1990 elections is undeniable: its vote, up 3% to 21%, caused hardly a dent in Labour's armour anywhere outside the north-east. The party's failure to carve out an urban municipal stronghold in the way that the Liberal Democrats have managed to do in the London borough of Tower Hamlets must be frustrating. Yet again it shows that however hard-pressed they may be, only a minority of working-class Scots look to the political world for redress, never mind salvation. The party has found it difficult to break down a sense of apathy and even demoralisation in Scottish working-class communities. When its star was briefly in the ascendant in the spring of 1989, Jim Sillars addressed a series of public meetings from Dalbeattie in Galloway to Aberdeen. The one he addressed in Glasgow's Castlemilk housing scheme received the most attention because at it he launched a swinging attack on Donald Dewar, but what was significant was that, in such a large catchment area, he could muster only forty-five people compared to the hundreds that turned out in rural Galloway and the north-east. At a time when the most regressive tax in many centuries was about to descend upon them, only a relative handful of working people could be roused from political torpor: this may confirm what committed leftists of differing hues have rarely faced up to, except upon renouncing their previous loyalties: that middle-class and even rural voters show far more inclination to engage in politics and even display political militancy, especially on an issue like environmental protection which is pushing its way to the top of the radical agenda.

The class consciousness for which Clydeside is famed has created a tolerance for radical political views which is not always found in traditional manufacturing regions elsewhere in the UK. But an actively politicised society has failed to emerge from Clydeside's much vaunted red traditions. Small things reveal this to be the case: the absence of political jokes to find a place in the gallery of irreverent working-class humour that Glasgow is famed for, despite the material provided by a succession of ill-conceived Thatcher visits which would have launched a thousand well-aimed gags if eastern Europe had been the scene of similar stage-managed episodes by the local party chief.

An insight into working-class priorities in Edinburgh was shown during 1988: an attempted Australian takeover of Scottish and Newcastle breweries produced a level of indignation among ordinary citizens that those engaged in seeking support for Nationalist projects such as the Constitutional Convention or Independence in Europe would dearly like to have been able to evoke. In September 1989, 72% of Scots had not heard of the Convention's existence.[10] This is testimony to the failure of those promoting an alternative form of Scottish government to reach out to ordinary voters and demonstrate its relevance to their lives. Admittedly the Convention strategists have been more concerned (perhaps with some cause) to mobilise the politically aware and the influential, but the failure of so many Scots to be aware of what has been treated as the most exciting constitutional initiative seen in Britain for many years is one that the status quo will no doubt exploit to the full.

Failure to engage the interest of those silent throngs beyond the intelligentsia or the already politically engaged is something that affects constitutional and separatist nationalists equally. Jim Sillars has reached out to a large part of the target audience for his brand of nationalist populism by writing a regular column in the *Sun* newspaper. Upon joining the SNP in 1981 Sillars quickly identified with the 79 Group faction which saw the main hope for radical change lying in the working class: it is doubtful whether then or now many of its members would have considered writing for the *Sun* as a means of consciousness-raising. The Group was proscribed and Alex Salmond, possibly its most gifted member, has gone on to create a parliamentary base in the rural seat of Banff and Buchan. Meanwhile, he has performed a service to the party by creating the

Scottish Centre for Economic and Social Research, a think-tank that will both firm up nationalist policy, particularly in the socio-economic sphere, and offer a platform for wide-ranging debate about the future of Scotland. This is not territory that the 79 Group would have regarded as naturally its own. It might have joined with Gordon Brown, editor of the *Red Paper on Scotland* in lamenting the fact that Scotland has 'no socialist book club, no socialist labour college . . . only a handful of socialist magazines and pamphlets'. But as the Marxist historian, Victor Kiernan, commented: 'If any large part of the working class wanted such things, Scotland would have them.'[11] Sam Coull, an ex-SNP councillor for Aberdeenshire, writing in *The Scotsman* in 1984, felt compelled to point out to Messrs Sillars and Salmond some characteristics of the Labour voter 'on which they have pinned a target':

> After fifteen years in the building trade, ten in the Post Office, and other contact with 'the target', I find he mostly buys the *Record, Sun,* or *Mirror*. His daily reading experience starts with the football at the back page, horses/dog results and today's runners next, then the used car prices, big girl on page three and finally, a glance at a front-page disaster photo coupled to a three-word headline and four column inches of story. He reads his newspaper in reverse and takes about ten minutes, sometimes less to do it.
>
> Conversation is confined to three topics – sport, sex, and last night's telly; only on rare occasions does politics intrude with tea-break chatter. When politics does become a topic, we invariably get treated to a regurgitation of what Kinnock, Healey, or the poor man's prophet, Wedgie Benn, was trying to get across on Sir Robin Day's show the night before.[12]

No revolution in the Scottish popular press has occurred to suggest that the reading habits of Sam Coull's workmates are any different in the early 1990s than they were in the mid-1980s. The relegation of politics as a subject of conversational interest comes from a sense of fatalism that there is not much powerless workers can do to alter the economic system or political structures that control their lives.

In the 1989 Glasgow Central by-election, it was possible to encounter many people leading demanding and impoverished lives for whom getting through each day was a struggle. For many of them Labour's comforting platitudes and the lusty tones of Denis Healey singing 'Molly Malone' while on the campaign stump were more consoling than the visionary appeal of the SNP's 'New Clydesiders' who had arrived to set them free, invoking the memory of Wheatley and Maxton. It may have escaped the SNP strategists that for people who cling to a precarious routine in order to get them through life, uncertainty is too much to handle and liberation can be a downright alarming prospect.

The authors of the novel, *No Mean City,* which gave the Gorbals district now lying in the Glasgow Central seat its notoriety, included in the book a radical figure, the brother of the violent gang leader Stark, whose striving for a better way through politics was depicted as being as futile as his brother's fixation with the razor.[13] This was written in 1935, during the Wheatley-Maxton era: even then, it was argued, politics was viewed as a fool's preoccupation unless some material attainment was being sought. Much in this depressing and cynical novel (whose main author ended his life not long after publication) is overdone, but depicting the pursuit of politics as being viewed as futile by many ordinary Glaswegians, may be a more accurate description of present-day realities than of earlier times.

The SNP has tried various means to increase its influence in Scottish working-class communities. The latest approach, which could be summed up as 'bash the ruling Labour Party', has not proved electorally rewarding. Nor has the cry that only in SNP hands is Scotland's future secure, a shrill note increasingly heard in the SNP repertoire. The indifference of voters to such appeals suggests that a less confrontational approach might bear more fruit.

In his chapter on 'The Lessons of Ireland', Bob Purdie advises Scottish Nationalists of the need to increase their awareness of internal realities in Scotland. The party chairman's 1990 New Year message, urging an East European type of popular revolution, suggested a pretty radical gulf in perception from on high.

Purdie offers the reminder that the single fact of sharing a status as subordinate nations does not mean that there was an automatic strategic or tactical consonance between Scotland and Ireland. But both drives for national self-determination have been bedevilled by sectarian religious factors: in Ulster they were such as to estrange the skilled working class completely from Irish nationalism; in Scotland sectarianism has proven to be episodic – not a state of permanent animosity and ongoing conflict. 'It emerges in specific situations and can lie dormant for long periods.'

At present it is dormant, as the current unsatisfactory relationship with England enables Scotland to derive coherence and unity as a nation in a way that it has not managed to do for many centuries. But in the event of a changed relationship with a dominant neighbour, brought about by self-government, the basis for unity will have to come from within; this means finding enough common ground between the various interests (including religious ones) that

define Scotland to contain differences and divergences that inevitably will become more apparent.

The tendency of the rival nationalisms in Ireland to look for
legitimacy from only one section of the island's population is a lesson
to be avoided in Scotland. Purdie also warns against Scots being
seduced by the superficial attractions of violence at any stage of their
self-determination struggle. He reckons that the Westminster
government's closing off of every avenue for constitutional redress of
Scotland's grievances closely parallels the situation which gave rise
to the civil rights movement in Northern Ireland in the late 1960s.
The civil rights leadership lacked the knowledge and experience to
sustain a non-violent strategy. If a struggle for justice in Scotland
does not obtain redress within existing constitutional arrangements,
'it will have to involve passive resistance and civil disobedience'.
Such an approach contains a potential for violence that will have to
be consciously resisted. 'If violence occurs the proponents of Scottish
self-government must ensure that it is inflicted *on* them and not *by*
them.'

Isobel Lindsay asks what is the most fruitful role that Scotland can
play in a Europe where ethnic strife is far from absent, but where it
is felt that the gravest threat to the self-realisation of individuals and
communities may lie in the unchecked use of corporate and
bureaucratic power by the European Community and those powerful economic interests that clearly stand to gain most from the
enactment of the Single European Act in 1992.

The SNP's flagship policy of 'Independence in Europe', which the
party conference enthusiastically adopted in 1988 after a long period
of equivocation on what should be its exact approach to the EC,
scarcely fills her with enthusiasm. Her chapter argues that given the
evolving shape of the EC, membership even as an independent state
is likely to produce in an enlarged context many of the problems
which have resulted in Scotland's dissatisfaction with the union.
With the bureaucratic centralism of the EC growing unchecked and
with the Single European Act, due for implementation in 1992, set to
concentrate economic power and impose growing standardisation,
the dangers to the viability and future distinctiveness of the smaller
nations and regions are as obvious as the opportunities for multi-
national corporations.

The need to be part of a process of 'modernisation', of being
associated with the important and the powerful, and of having seats
at the top table partly explain the rise of Euro-nationalism within the
SNP. It comes through clearly in policy-statements and particularly
in the comments of party members defending the policy in the press
and elsewhere. I am reminded of the uncomfortable thought that

the same compulsion to extricate Scotland from the status of provincial economic backwater drove her into the Union and later drew some of her brightest and most energetic sons into imperial service for two centuries. They were not overly concerned with the nature of the power structures that they were maintaining, nor with the effects of such involvements on the cultural distinctiveness of Scotland and it is possible to detect a similar unconcern with the small print of the emergent EC super-state on the part of nationalist enthusiasts for Europe: accordingly these Europhiles should not be surprised if their commitment to genuine participatory democracy and the protection of Scottish culture appears to be questioned by those who feel that small-state nationalism is primarily about bringing control nearer to ordinary citizens.

The lustre of EC membership for many Nationalists also stems from the belief that the Community may offer a quick escape route that renders unnecessary the need to reach a prior settlement with England. But here too Isobel Lindsay counsels caution: a majority of Scottish MPs and MEPs favouring Independence in Europe would constitute a moral mandate but not an unstoppable power base. In order to prevail a united front of Scottish popular and institutional interests would need to be created in order to add force to the mandate; unfortunately, the SNP's recent record in such cross-party initiative does not suggest that the party realises their importance or could easily set them in motion if the need arose.

The credibility of the idea that there is an easy way to break free from the constricting Scottish-English relationship is not enhanced by the air of ruthlessness and determination to defend state interests conveyed by the Thatcher government: however ill-conceived its policies there is none of the irresolution associated with government in the 1970s which instilled hope in Nationalist hearts that the Scottish leap forward could be quick and painless. Among ordinary Scottish voters, the June 1989 European Elections showed that no feeling of the shrinking power of United Kingdom government exists, ready to put wind in the sails of the SNP's Euro flagship.

As the thirteenth member of the EC, Isobel Lindsay reckons that Scotland would have scarcely more influence or discretion in key economic areas than is the case now. Indeed, if Independence in Europe is seen primarily as a means of influencing EC decisions, there is no clear-cut advantage separating independence and a democratic Scottish parliament in a federal United Kingdom.

Scotland's own experience of long-distance rule ought to incline it towards an anti-integration position, favouring the Europe of the Nations and the Regions rather than a Franco-German inspired West European super-state. The need to value locally based democratic responsibility over long-distance dependency (even if the pill is sweetened by much benign patronage) is a good basis for a Scottish approach to internationalism. Ordinary citizens are not likely to have much long-term security or regular access to decision-making in a multi-national political conglomerate that is dominated from the inside track by the professional lobbyist, the bureaucrat, the career politician, and the industrial mogul. The example of the Soviet Union already points to the stultifying effects of concentrating power at the centre, creating massive institutions with little public account-ability, pushing mass standardisation rather than diversification.

Isobel Lindsay reckons that Scotland's natural geo-physical position makes her part of the 'top storey' of the common European home. This top storey encompasses Iceland, the Scandinavian countries, the Baltic states, and the rest of the North West Soviet Union. Early modern Scotland had close links of trade and migration with many of these countries. There is also a shared concern with the need to allow voluntaristic patterns of inter-state relations to develop and to develop pan-European structures that will provide a forum for conflict resoluton, security issues, and ecological co-operation.

The mainstream SNP has been curiously insular and complacent about cultivating mutually reinforcing ties with groups and organisation in Europe and further afield which have the same aims. In 1990 the party went largely unrepresented at the Prague launch of the Helsinki Citizens Assembly, an attempt to create a permanent citizens' forum composed of peace, environmental, and human rights groups which would be a counter-force against the power-brokers attempting to determine the shape of the new Europe. Its attempt to mobilise the radicalism of eastern Europe on its own behalf is rather counterfeit when it is so removed from initiatives like the Citizens Assembly, which pool experiences and enable contacts to be established between the two halves of Europe.

In 1989 the chief foreign guests at the SNP conference were the leaders in the European Parliament of the ruling Irish party, Fianna Fail, which long ago buried a reforming nationalist image in order to make its peace with multi-national capital and preside over large-scale migration. Such connections and the decision of Winifred Ewing, the SNP's only Euro MP to sit with the centralist French Gaullists for ten years, have given Scottish nationalism a poor image in the eyes of other movements championing the cause of stateless nations.

When a Scottish delegation attended the inaugural conference of European Youth Nationalists in Bilbao during 1986, they were distressed to find that the prevalent view of the SNP was that of a conservative movement which, at Strasbourg, entered into cynical relationships with French chauvinist parties like the Gaullists mainly because of a shared anti-English bias. At this and succeeding Young Nationalists conferences in Barcelona and the Pyrennees, the radical Scottish contingent managed to repair the damage. But it is note-worthy that a party so keen to emerge from the shadow of the English colossus in order to re-engage with the wider world, has been unable to put these sentiments into practice. Even the Labour Party in Scotland has a better record of achievement: it has built up credibility as internationalist and radical by its championing of the Sandinista cause in Nicaragua which culminated in a visit to Scotland by Daniel Ortega, the former Nicaraguan President, in 1989.

It would not involve a great outlay of enthusiasm or expenditure for the SNP to make good this deficiency. In his New Year message, party chairman Gordon Wilson linked Scotland with the re-awakened nationalism of eastern Europe, a high-risk course given the chauvinistic character of some of the emergent movements. But there is no sign that the SNP has been to the fore in making common cause even with the relatively benign examples of reawakened nationalism in eastern Europe, such as the movement for self-determination in each of the Baltic States. Scots could have used their traditionally close ties with the Soviet Union in order to urge restraint on Moscow: such an appeal might not have cut much ice, but it would have been an example of practical solidarity that might have evoked a warm response in beleaguered Lithuania.

Enlightened self-interest might conceivably have persuaded SNP MPs at Westminster to ask Mrs Thatcher to reconsider her opposi-tion to Scottish self-government in light of the crisis in the Baltic States. Soviet unwillingness to concede the demands of popularly based Baltic nationalists stemmed from a growing irritation that in the new Europe it was they who were having to make all the con-cessions and adjustments while the West sat back with arms folded, blissfully unaware of the acute democratic shortcomings in its own society. To appease the majority sentiment in the subordinate kingdom of the realm by conceding a locally based parliament with substantial powers is a gesture that would surely not have gone unnoticed in Moscow and might have strengthened Gorbachev's hand against his own hardliners. But the SNP's attachment to a purist strategy of 'Independence nothing less' ruled out such a mischievous course.

Most sections of the party have also been numb to the idea that a decentralised Europe of the regions could prove to be a more accept-able buffer against the excesses of a potential supra-national state than existing nation-states, many of which do not inspire the loyalty that regional attachments produce among many Europeans. The Europe of the regions is a concept that inspires many of the fourteen stateless nations represented at the European Young Nationalist gatherings who are aware that outright statehood is beyond their reach and may not be the most desirable option available to them. It is a concept that could inspire ethnic minorities oppressed under communism who are too interspersed across the mountains and plains of central and eastern Europe to be able to form coherent nation-states. Young Scots at the European nationalist conventions found that they were rather out on a limb in their attachment to full-blown independence just as their party has been at home.

Much of the SNP's dogmatism in the 1980s (summed up by the slogan 'Independence Nothing Less') was a reaction to the Thatcher years when meaningful self-government within a reformed British state seemed completely beyond reach. In the wake of Thatcher's departure a reaction is likely to set in against her bruising adversarial style of politics. It would be an error of judgment for the SNP not to realise the context in which its own fundamentalism has evolved and the need for the party to adopt a more co-operative and inclusive approach without sacrificing its principles. Failure to adapt to different political conditions may leave it stranded, in tone and posture a reminder of the embattled and sectarian Thatcher years which her own party is already keen to distance itself from. So the 1990s are likely to require an adaptable, fast-moving party keen to exploit local grievances and make the connections with the absence of accountable government in Scotland. If a leader like Alex Salmond fails to lift the party from the trough it has found itself in since 1979, then it is hard to see how it can emerge as a serious contender for power in Scotland.

3

Nationalism, Journalism and Cultural Politics

CHRISTOPHER HARVIE

In September 1990 Welsh nationalism was riven by a spectacular culture clash. At Machynlleth on Saturday 15, the Rev. R. S. Thomas, the greatest living Anglo-Welsh poet, denounced the leader of Plaid Cymru, Dafydd Elis Thomas, for selling out the Welsh language, and commended a group called the Covenanters of a Free Wales, who wanted to placard cottages bought by English people in Welsh Wales, telling them to go home. The implication being that if they took Dafydd El along with them, so much the better.

For the next few days the Welsh papers ran stories featuring the poet, who was ritually denounced by Welsh politicians of all hues, but – even from the Tory Secretary of State – more in regret than in anger: a would-be monoglot Lear roaring in grief and pain from the Llyn peninsula. Bernard Levin had recently been pontificating on the Welsh language in *The Times*, and among most Welsh people, I'd judge, it was reckoned better to be wrong with Thomas than right with Levin.[1]

Only a few weeks earlier an incident had occurred in Scotland which provides an interesting contrast. With the death of his widow Valda in 1989, the cottage of Hugh MacDiarmid at Brownsbank near Biggar became tenantless, and George Galloway MP raised the question of preserving it as a memorial in a letter to the Secretary of State. He received a reply from the office of Ian Lang, then the Housing Minister, thanking him for drawing Mr MacDiarmid's housing problems to his attention, and saying that the Minister would give these due consideration. A howler of this magnitude got a mention in *The Scotsman* diary, and nothing more. Which might mean that people had given up hoping for rational argument from a government whose esteem had sunk to pitiful levels; or that, in comparison to Wales, culture hadn't mattered all that much in the nationalist revival.

Another occasion rich in ambiguity was the death of Norman

Buchan MP, whose attitude to home rule was, to put it mildly, sceptical. Yet Buchan's knowledge of Scots poetry, drama and folk-song was not just extensive in itself; as a Communist and inter-nationalist he had consciously deployed it in the 1940s and 1950s to make it part of Scottish radicalism. I remember him prowling round a Fabian conference on devolution in Perth in 1978, grumbling about the lack of interest of any of the delegates present in anything to do with culture, before settling on me for a flyting with a 'I suppose you'll have to do' expression on his face.

He was not alone in lamenting the a-cultural quality of Scottish nationalism in the 1970s. Meetings of the Scottish National Party lacked both kilts and literary figures, in contrast to the apparent situation before World War II.[2] Writers and artists, however nationalist in sympathy, shied from a party so explicitly 'modernising' in its ethos and, despite the literary enthusiasm of the chairman, William Wolfe, this distrust was reciprocated by many leading figures in the party. Norman MacCaig, interviewed by Conor Cruise O'Brien in a TV programme in 1979, said that he would always vote SNP, but didn't believe an independent Scotland would be very exhilarating to live in.

In one of several studies of the SNP published during the decade, Dr Jack Brand, a former Labour Party man who had turned nationalist, commented that although literature may have mobilised members of the party élite – and was interesting for this reason – the intellectual trend in Scotland had really been away from nationalism towards socialism.[3] Paradoxically, Brand argued, this aided SNP organisation. Political mobilisation did not conflict with an existing scale of literary values – or with literary nationalists throwing their weight around.[4]

The rapid decline of the SNP after 1978, the year in which Brand's book was published, fractured its aura of competent non-ideological modernisation, as well as that of the political scientists who bought its line. But the 1980s saw a nationalist stance become general among the Scottish intelligentsia, before the SNP vote recovered to 1970s levels after the 1987 elections. The orthodoxy is now that the revival in painting, film and the novel, in poetry and drama – staged and televised – kept a 'national movement' in being. The activists – mainly literary, religious, journalistic and academic – who noted the novelist Alasdair Gray's injunction in 1982 Janine (1985) to work 'as if you were in the early days of a better nation' and sustained the Campaign for a Scottish Assembly through several discouraging years, until the Constitutional Convention first met, invoke parallels far beyond the Scottish community, notably with the Civic Forum or New Forum type of organisation, rather similarly composed, which helped destabilise Communist East Europe.[5] When the Labour Party's delegates to the Constitutional Convention preferred the 'pluralism' of a Scottish parliament elected by proportional representation (in which their majority would be uncertain) to the virtual dictatorship in towns like Glasgow which the first-past-the-post system gave them, they were, in a sense, surrendering a 'leading role of the party' which they had exercised for over half a century.

The success of other citizens' movements organised by the intelligentsia has presented a plausible answer to the taunts of social and economic irrelevance flung by Conservatives at home rule activists. But the critical factor in propelling Labour to enter the Convention was the revival of the SNP's fortunes, and the threat that after the Govan election it posed to Labour in its heartlands. Even when the party was in eclipse, approval of its goal – independence – increased dramatically. The trend since 1945 (when this issue was first analysed) must have worried Labour as well as most Unionists, as separatist feelings seemed little less strong among Labour voters than among SNP supporters.[6]

	1945	1965-1974	1988	1990
Independence	8	22	33	38
Devolution	53	63	42	42
Status Quo	39	15	25	20

Changes in public opinion which do not involve party activity (all parties seem to have lost activists during the 1980s) and the success of *ad hoc* groups like the Convention, or the various anti-poll tax organisations, forces us to reconsider the scepticism about literary action of Brand and, writing in 1968, Harry Hanham.

Hanham's *Scottish Nationalism* was, perhaps, over-indulgent to the printed word, and granted a particular phase to 'literary nationalism', from the MacDiarmid-inspired 'Scottish renaissance' of the early 1920s, to the eviction of the *literati* from the new SNP after 1934.[7] Of SNP policy after World War II Hanham wrote that its 'most significant feature' was 'the total omission of a section on Scottish culture':

> Writers are read by the sort of man the SNP programme was intended to win only when they write about his culture convincingly and sentimentally (the *Sunday Post* published in Dundee catches the tone exactly). When they write about things beyond the ken of small-town man they are not read at all.[8]

Even with the growth of support for nationalism in the late 1980s, the suspicion still lingered that the SNP's attitude to culture continued to run along the grooves of the Dundee Press. At the

Govan election campaign several political intellectuals, the present writer among them, broke with old Labour loyalties to support Jim Sillars. Rather more claimed, after he had won, that Sillars was indeed the 'man of destiny'. They were dismayed when Sillars then encouraged the SNP to boycott the Convention, and even in 1990 the party probably attracted rather less intellectual confidence than the Scottish TUC, whose General Secretary, Campbell Christie, was an astute cultural diplomat; or the hard-working members of the by now miniscule Communist Party with their 'What's Left?' cultural weekends.

Matters may change with the election of Alex Salmond as SNP convener: less because Salmond is in any sense a literary intellectual but because he comes from a sector of Scottish society – the universities and the banking world – which has a strong vested interest in the country's 'post-industrial' intellectual capital. During a period when inward investment depends to a very great extent on the quality both of training and cultural life that can be offered, a sensitive political leadership gains by being open and sympathetic to intellectuals' *démarches*.

Intellectual ambiguity about nationalism is of long duration, although historical writing about it is only recent. While Hanham expressed his indebtedness to Dr George Elder Davie, he did not explore Davie's contention that the low profile of nationalism was due to explicit campaigns of Anglicisation during the nineteenth century, which sapped the foundations of the country's 'democratic intellect'.[9] Davie emphasised in a Weberian way the influence of culture on political movements, even if its overall effect was negative. The same theme was taken up by two more Marxist commentators of the 1970s, Tom Nairn in *The Break-up of Britain* and the present writer in *Scotland and Nationalism* (both 1977). We argued that intellectual 'assimilationism' and imperialism, after the 'premature modernisation' of the Enlightenment, disadvantaged nationalism; but also that the desire to liberate themselves from the ethos of a crumbling empire would, sooner or later, alter social attitudes.[10] Nairn was the more schematic in rooting an intellectual deformation in changing class formation. I tended to attribute assimilation to the political breakdown in the early nineteenth century which culminated in the disruption of the Church of Scotland in 1843, engendering a sterile, sectarian conflict from which constructively-minded intellectuals fled. In Nairn's view a mature capitalism on a British scale absorbed the eccentric Scottish intellectual advance; in mine, a sequence of political reverses ended the prospect of effective autonomy. But both of us had got the notion of Scots 'mission' from our old Marxist contagion: the peculiarities – and indeed the opportunities – of the country's politics were to do with its position in a developmental process.

In accounting both for the eclipse of Scottish nationalism in the nineteenth century, and the reversal of this process in the twentieth, the increasing intellectual input which has steadily throttled non-nationalist interpretations, both Nairn and I depended on Gramsci's notion of the balance of 'organic' and 'traditional' intelligentsias. Like Marx, Gramsci saw political *praxis* occurring where intellectual 'understanding' combined with the desperation of the proletariat. Arguing to some extent from Britain in 1848, where the intellectuals inhibited rather than furthered revolutionary change, he divided them into two: an 'organic' intelligentsia who were essentially the experts of the industrial economy, whose ethic could affect the proletariat in the course of its work; and a 'traditional' intelligentsia which, in education, law and medicine, served the conservative order.[11] The latter *can* change (its commitment to 'values' may even make it – or some of its members – a radical force in a crisis) but it usually influences the less focused 'organic' intellectuals in a conservative direction.

I argued in *Scotland and Nationalism* that during the Enlightenment the traditional intelligentsia – clergy, lawyers, and landowners – pre-empted the functions of the organic intelligentsia. Their expertise in the social sciences, invention and entrepreneurship, thus inoculated the country against any awkward radicalism on the part of this group.[12] But this process did not end with 'mature' industrialisation. If we analyse a representative group of twentieth-century Scottish writers – I have used those who appear in the appendix of Roderick Watson's *The Literature of Scotland* (thirty-seven in all) – then out of this number, at the beginning of their careers, seven were from the 'old' professions, medicine, law, the church, and only five from the 'new intelligentsia' of industrial society; but twenty-three, or nearly two-thirds, were either journalists or teachers.[13]

But where, in Gramsci's categories, do journalists and teachers fit? Journalists are 'organic'. They are part of 'print capitalism'. But they are 'traditional' in being directed by politicians often loyal to 'pre-industrial' parties. Teachers are 'organic': part of a system producing an adaptive and obedient work-force, but they have also a 'traditional' corporate identity which transmits values either of the old order – or even those held by the teacher him- or herself. Such cultural conditioners of nationalism have exerted an important long-term effect, both by direct political interventions and by influencing the way the Scottish populace identifies itself. Does this overthrow even the Gramscian notion of base-superstructure relations, replacing it with neo-liberal notions of the autonomy of ideas, and the ways in which they are 'marketed' by the increasingly sophisticated machinery of press and media? And, if this is the case, is Scotland a specific case of 'bourgeois regionalism': a happy combination of media expertise with lavish natural resources, but with nothing in particular to say to the modern world?

When Edwin Muir wrote of Glasgow being closer to other industrial cities than to the rest of Scotland, he acknowledged the social and economic patterns which produced a notably cosmopolitan 'organic intelligentsia'.[14] Glasgow was the world centre of shipbuilding and the iron trade, whose dominant groups – and their Labour opponents – were part of a global economic network. The *Glasgow Herald*'s annual 'Trade and Industry' supplement was *the* authority on shipbuilding; while Clydeside industrial militancy after the 1906-7 depression was linked both to American urban radicalism and to 'cosmopolitan' South Wales. Neither bourgeoisie nor proletariat had much time for the parochial-nationalist pabulum of Victorian Scotland; at the same time the absence of any sort of functioning *polis* meant that their political competence was curiously deformed. A 'MacAndrew's Hymn' compound of technology and pietism left little space for social speculation until the end of the century. When radicalism came, the Glasgow bourgeoisie's artistic *avant-gardism* would foreshadow the rise of an international market in contemporary art; while Glasgow Marxism was aggressively internationalist. Both were utopian in their future-orientation and, in the *literal* meaning of that word, not specific as to place.

   Fin-de-siècle nationalism was antiquarian and querulous. A modernising ideology like that of Sinn Féin in Ireland, or the inter-war SNP, was only fitfully present. Even where nationalists and progressives linked up, as in *Forward*, edited by Tom Johnston and largely financed by Roland Eugene Muirhead, they had different priorities. Labour's most constructive thinker, the Catholic John Wheatley, a regular *Forward* contributor, was agnostic about home rule; Johnston switched it on whenever he needed an increased subvention from Muirhead.[15]

   Penalised by his dourness, Muirhead was still the nearest Scotland came to a progressive nationalist: an anti-imperialist, converted to nationalism when he went as a leather merchant and tanner to small states in South America, whose organisation he hoped Scotland would emulate.[16] Similar experiences had attracted the most romantic of the radical leaders, 'Don Roberto' Cunninghame-Graham, to the cause. But despite Graham's distinguished prose style, and the informed interest in politico-economic relationships which he contributed to his friend Joseph Conrad's *Nostromo*, the picture of Scotland conveyed by his writings was distinctly elegaic, tinged with the melancholy of a landowner who realised that his class's time had passed.[17]

In the late Victorian period, the assimilationist alternative was often an imperial one: the route taken by John Buchan, for example. But this could mean an acquaintance with colonial self-government, and with imperial-federationist ideas which promoted home rule. The Borders farmer turned London store-director, F. S. Oliver, in 1911-14 proposed a federal system as his solution to the Irish crisis: something that may have influenced the subsequent attitudes of his friend Buchan.[18] Also involved imperially were Lord Pentland (Scottish Secretary, 1906-11) and, in a host of town plans for India, Palestine and Egypt, his *protégé* Patrick Geddes, an enthusiastic Celtic revivalist in the 1890s who encouraged the young Mac-Diarmid in his nationalist aims at the end of World War I.[19]

'Optimists' could cite the imperial role as an argument for a recognised partnership, with Scotland in a role similar to that of the states federated, over the previous fifty years, into Canada, Australia and South Africa. But this conflicted with politicians – Scots as well as carpet-baggers – who wanted a disproportionate share of the central power at Westminster, and with the fact that most Conservatives did not, like Cecil Rhodes, regard home rule for Ireland as a step towards imperial federation, but as a dissolving agent.[20] Such apprehension and complacency underlay the attitudes of most of the Kailyarders, who regarded English nonconformity, literary politics and the empire as fair fields of action and resented anything which might get in their way.

By contrast the 'pessimists' who reacted against this complacency often identified their liberal fellow-countrymen as the villains, something which was unlikely to encourage self-government and could endorse the right-wing, assimilationist views of such as J. Hepburn Miller in his *Literary History of Scotland* (1903). George Douglas Brown, in *The House with the Green Shutters* (1900), John MacDougall Hay in *Gillespie* (1913) and the young John Buchan expressed at least an agnosticism about self-government, on the grounds that this would prolong the dominance of third-rate Kailyard politicians.

Here, such 'modernising' critique of Scottish society as was articulated came from the traditional intelligentsia. The 'organic' intelligentsia was divided – politically, religiously and spatially (much of it having emigrated). There was no 'new Liberalism' of the sort that energised the English provinces, partly because there was no 'Scottish Question'; moreover, in a predominantly Liberal country, the 'serious press' which had to project it was Unionist.

'The writers of Newspapers, Pamphlets, Poems, Books, these *are* the real working effective Church of a modern country.'[21] Carlyle, himself exemplifying what happened to an intelligentsia when its *polis* dissolved, emphasised the salience of journalists in Scottish cultural life in the nineteenth century. Following the assault on the metropolis by the *Edinburgh Reviewers* and their Tory rivals at *Blackwood's Magazine*, the likes of J. D. Cook, editing the *Saturday Review*, Sir Thomas Wemyss Reid and Sir Robert Donald on the *Daily News* dominated the middle-class press, probably because the arts of rhetoric, précis and didactics were taught at Scottish universities and not at Oxford or Cambridge.[22] The importance of this has been stressed by Dr William Donaldson in *Popular Literature in Victorian Scotland* (1986), a book which has revolutionised our notion of the Scots literary community, by shifting attention away from the book to the enormous amount of fiction and social commentary, frequently in the vernacular, published in the Scottish press.[23] But this liveliness had lapsed by World War I, as Scottish papers emulated the sensationalism and trivialisation of Northcliffe's 'new journalism'.[24] In England such schoolmasterly, political figures were being evicted both by young dons flocking to the serious papers from the old universities – that stream of impressive initials: L. T. Hobhouse, H. J. Massingham, C. E. Montague, etc. – and by the 'cockneys' of the sensationalist 'new journalism'. Although T. W. H. Crosland accused the 'unspeakable Scot' of having polluted metropolitan journalism, he seems increasingly to have been excluded from it.[25]

The Scottish press preserved the older – pre-Harmsworth – English order, with a substantial proportion of middle-class papers sponsoring a conservative, rather parochial, but still Scottish ethos. Locked like this, the 'nationalist' journalist had to escape – notably by using the pseudonym. There are nineteenth-century precedents: 'Christopher North', 'Bon Gaultier', 'The Author of Waverley' himself. But in the twentieth century this became a recognised tactic. Neil Munro, editor of the *Glasgow Herald*, had a demotic doppelgänger, Hugh Foulis, creator of Para Handy and Erchie Shaw. In the inter-war period the numbers multiplied. 'Hugh MacDiarmid' and 'Lewis Grassic Gibbon' were the most famous coinages, but

J. M. Reid, the editor of the Conservative *Bulletin*, wrote for nationalist periodicals as Colin Walkinshaw and George Malcolm Thomson turns up under a variety of aliases.[26] Does the pseudonym, however, indicate a malfunctioning political system, an over-elaboration of the printed word? When Scottish politics took on its own momentum, after 1960, it seems to have disappeared.[27]

There was also the alternative, taken by Carlyle himself, of compounding with the devil and moving south. Despite lacklustre MPs, Scots have always provided a disproportionate number of Westminster political commentators: in our own day Robert Carvel, James Margach, Ian Aitken, James Naughtie, and John Lloyd. It's possible to find Scots publicists – in the retinue of Rupert Murdoch or the Adam Smith Institute – whose rejection of the possibility of any Scots *polis* seems total: Andrew Neil, Dr Madsen Pirie, and so on. The English 'open élite' has always attracted its open élitists – even from Catholic Ireland – as J. L. Garvin, Brendan Bracken, Dr Patrick Cosgrove and John O'Sullivan have proved.

'The Condition of Scotland Question', however, exists in a sense that it never did in Carlyle's day, or indeed before 1918. World War I had an impact in Scotland far beyond what it had in Britain as a whole. As MacDiarmid later wrote:

> It took the full force of the War to jolt an adequate majority of the Scottish people out of their old mental, moral and material ruts.[28]

There were few moments of glory, plenty of above-average casualty lists.[29] Heavy industry was reorganised and increased in capacity, the resistance of Clydeside skilled workers to 'dilution' was overcome by a mixture of concession (rent control) and coercion (jailing political and union activists). Such government action pro-voked socialist organisation on the Clyde in the last two years of the war. It stagnated or declined elsewhere in Britain, but seemed justified when the post-war boom ended in 1921 and unemploy-ment moved towards 20%.

In fact this depression did not boost the Left, whose successes in November 1922 were won against a background of falling Labour Party membership and dwindling fortunes in local politics. John MacLean was less influential in 1923 than he had been in 1918. But it hit the confidence of Scottish business and its 'organic intelligentsia', with echoes which still reverberated thirty years later, as the economist Andrew Cairncross found:

> Recollection of those days still exerts a powerful influence. A strong sense of long-term insecurity remains, and plays an

important part in production, politics, conversation and almost every other aspect of life. Hostile suspicion often flares up in reaction to proposals in which there is any hint of labour redundancy.[30]

Some industrial leaders were ingested into the Whitehall machine as authorities and advisers; others found themselves isolated, like the Fraserburgh fish-merchant family of the poet George Bruce who read themselves into Soviet Communism, trying to retrieve a vanished market. A class reared on free trade and non-intervention was in near despair. Even Sir Montague Norman, the conservative head of the Bank of England, the lender of last resort to much of Scots heavy industry, was appalled at the pessimism of Scots businessmen over their prospects.[31]

This 'national problem' gripped commentators from the mid-1920s on. The Left had of course always expressed social-critical views, but their Scottish context had been a marginal factor. However, after the failure of the first Labour government in 1924 and the rejection of Bills for Scottish devolution, the Left route looked much less promising. This spurred militant nationalists in the Scots National League, 'the first organisation to advocate complete independence for Scotland',[32] and started a journalistic mechanism, in which the broadcasting of the 'Scottish problem' was the work both of Scottish literary men and their organisations, and the sympathetic action of London press and publishing. Key dates are the founding by Muirhead of the Scottish Secretariat in 1924, the Scottish National League's Scots Independent in 1926, and the first metropolitan articulation of Scottish nationalism in the same year.[33]

A publishing executive at Kegan Paul seems to have caused this by commissioning a series of short polemical works, largely by radical authors who had worked for that demanding training school, A. R. Orage's New Age. In 1926, a young Oxford-educated journalist, George Malcolm Thomson, published Caledonia, or the Future of the Scots, in which he voiced the fears of the Scottish bourgeoisie about Irish immigration – 'The gravest race problem of any nation in Europe today', English chain stores: trebled since 1918; Scottish slums: 'A malignant disease affecting the whole body of the nation'.[34] Thomson advocated home rule but his conclusions, here and in a later volume, The Rediscovery of Scotland, were deeply pessimistic – he forecast a religious civil war in the 1980s.[35] But he then played a leading part in persuading Lord Beaverbrook (himself Scots in origin) to establish the Scottish Daily Express in Glasgow in 1930, with a devolutionist slant to its politics.[36]

Hugh MacDiarmid, writing as C. M. Grieve, published Albyn, or Scotland and the Future in the same series in the following year.

Adapted from articles he had written for Muirhead's Scottish
Secretariat (which were then syndicated throughout Scottish local
newspapers) and owing much to his *Contemporary Scottish Cultural
Studies*, then appearing as essays in the *Scottish Educational Journal*,
this voiced much the same pessimism as Thomson. Grieve wrote:

> The outlook is exceedingly grave . . . our race and culture are
> faced with a peril which, though silent and unostentatious, is
> the gravest with which the Scottish people have ever been
> confronted.[37]

Devolution was dismissed as 'the last step in the assimilation of
Scotland to England'; the answer – if answer there was – lay in
Spengler's commendation of the smaller European countries as the
rescuers of the declining West (Grieve was particularly influenced by
the example of Norway, which had been completely independent for
only two decades), and in the Social Credit economics of Major C. H.
Douglas, Scots by birth and an obsession of Orage at the *New Age*.

In *No Gods and Precious Few Heroes* I stressed the non-national
element in the renaissance. Its concentration on personal liberation,
sexual and social, went hand in hand with the process of language
expansion which MacDiarmid derived from Joyce and applied to the
Scots vernacular.[38] But it was difficult to locate *praxis* in Scotland:
situations such like that confluence of talent which brought Grieve,
Edwin Muir, Francis George Scott and Tom MacDonald (Fionn
MacColla) to Montrose in 1926-27 were rare. For most, the way of
liberation led away from Scotland. Edwin and Willa Muir spent part
of the 1920s in Germany, as did A. S. Neill; Naomi Mitchison and
the Carswells were based in London, Grassic Gibbon in Welwyn
Garden City. Even MacColla and Grieve made their way south in
1930, with disastrous consequences for the latter.

In itself, the direct impact of Scottish renaissance poetry was
limited; MacDiarmid's *Sangschaw* collection, though armed with a
foreword by John Buchan, sold only just over one hundred copies in
its first year, and it's doubtful if even *A Drunk Man Looks at the
Thistle* reached more than the statutory 2,000.[39] On the other hand
Grieve's *Contemporary Scottish Studies* would reach upwards of
30,000 when carried in the *Scottish Educational Journal*, and when
the Scottish press began to carry his, and others', poems, they would
reach between 60,000 and 120,000 as far as the larger cities were
concerned. Hence the upbraiding of journalists for falling standards
was a major feature of *Contemporary Scottish Studies*, and one
which appears to have had some success.

The 1920s was a decade of change – largely positive – in Scottish
newspapers. Buchan, ever sensitive to social change, put a press
baron at the centre of his *Castle Gay* in 1930, and made a young

left-wing journalist, Dougal Crombie, a symbol of the Scottish future. Declining local prosperity and competition from wireless and cinema led to a fall in the number of titles and the amalgamation of competing papers in some of the cities. This produced in Dundee the Conservative Thomson-Leng organisation whose folksy weeklies, the *Sunday Post,* the *People's Friend* and *The Weekly News* were saturating the Scottish market by the 1930s. Stultifying though this was in some respects, many journalists admitted that the training given in the non-union printing house in Dundee was unparalleled.[40] By the end of the decade Beaverbrook's incursion into Glasgow, with a daily and an evening, had stirred up the press scene in the west. This enabled 'condition of Scotland' writing to exert increasing influence in the following years.

The implications of this for nationalism were ambiguous: it was frowned on, but less than it had been under the old order, and a lot less than socialism.[41] It was always 'good copy' for the papers challenging the hegemony of *The Scotsman* and the *Glasgow Herald.* 'From 1931 to 1934,' Brand writes, 'it was difficult to avoid the home rule issue if one read a Scottish newspaper.'[42] Under John MacCormick, the National Party of Scotland, formed in 1928, was quick to take advantage of such publicity. In 1928, MacCormick ran Cunninghame-Graham for the Rectorship of Glasgow University and he nearly beat Baldwin. This put the new party on the map, particularly among young Scots who would go on to teach or write for Scottish papers.[43] Against Hanham's charge of NPS ineffective-ness, Cunninghame-Graham's near-victory attracted 3,500 to a celebration rally in Glasgow's St Andrew's Halls, addressed by Grieve, MacCormick and the Duke of Montrose. Compton Mackenzie, also present, went on to win the Rectorship for the NPS in 1931,[44] by which time NPS membership had risen from 3,000 to 8,000 over one year.[45]

Many nationalists, MacDiarmid included, saw subsequent events as a betrayal of this promising beginning. In 1934, after negotiations between Neil Gunn of the NPS and George Malcolm Thomson of the Scottish Party, the Scottish National Party was formed. MacDiarmid was excluded by MacCormick, who continued as secretary, and Muirhead was marginalised. Besides MacDiarmid's personal problems, the blows of this political exclusion and of Edwin Muir's attack in *Scott and Scotland* (1936) on the very foundations of the literary movement he had started, were deeply hurtful.

The 1934 negotiations were aided by a split in the ranks of the Liberal Party between the 'Nationals' of Sir Godfrey Collins

(Secretary of State in 1932) and free traders.[46] There was also an 'imperialist' secession from the Unionist Party in the Glasgow constituency of Cathcart, fomented in part by Beaverbrook's *Scottish Daily Express*. Something of the chaos of that time is conveyed by Eric Linklater's *Magnus Merriman* (1934) which drew on his own experiences as NPS candidate in the East Fife by-election in 1933. The novel drew the attention of a metropolitan public to Scottish nationalism, but it also exposed its weaknesses. Moreover, the merger attempted to fuse incompatibles, the Liberal-imperialist 'home-rule-all-rounders', and the Muirheads and MacDiarmids with their yen for Sinn Féin in Ireland and the National Congress in India. SNP membership then declined steeply after 1934, until by the 1942 split it had barely 1,600 members.

'Literary nationalism' ended in apparent failure, its goals frustrated, MacDiarmid broken. But the 'Scottish question' *was* now practical politics, however much diagnoses might differ. Comparisons with small European states like Sweden and Norway had become part of the political vocabulary. The irony was that such journalism marginalised the linguistic component of MacDiarmid's programme. A disjunction remained between the vernacular of the lyric and the English that MacDiarmid himself used for his economic and social propaganda. Both he and Edwin Muir, for example, adopted Social Credit as a solution to Scotland's industrial problems, but MacDiarmid thought no more than Muir of using Lallans to argue for them, something which can't have been lost on Muir when he came to write *Scott and Scotland* in 1936.[47]

In the early 1930s literary nationalism exerted a twofold influence. MacDiarmid mobilised a younger generation to reassess their cultural fields against the national experience – philosophy with George Davie, Gaelic with Sorley MacLean.[48] He also added, in his Communist phase, the 'myth' of John MacLean as a symbol of Scottish revolutionary socialism. The penumbra projected by MacDiarmid's work in his last two decades – a fricative force, unlike the deep shadow cast by W. B. Yeats in Ireland – was not just a tribute to his poetry, but showed those investments paying off in Davie's *Democratic Intellect*, MacLean's revival of Gaelic poetry and the John MacLean cult of the younger socialists and nationalists. The irony of this radicalism, however, was that it was almost completely generated by the 'traditional' intelligentsia.

The second influence is much wider and more diffuse: the demand for a reassessment of Scotland's status within the UK, and for political mechanisms which would compensate for the southward drift of control. In 1932 John Buchan, now Unionist member for the Scottish universities, stood up (in a qualified way) against the assault on home rule made by the Scottish business community. (Ramsay MacDonald, reverting in his dotage to the first cause he had adopted, had spoken in its favour.) If the Scots wanted home rule they should have it, he argued, even if it didn't do them any good. His conclusion was an admission by a leading Unionist propagandist that the current assimilation was too fast.[49] Within four years similar views were being voiced by the National Liberal Secretary of State, Sir Godfrey Collins:

> Scotland's industries are not drifting, they are being dragged south. If Scottish businessmen had as much patriotism as they profess at Burns suppers and Bannockburn celebrations there would not be such a tale.[50]

Sir James Lithgow, who as a shipbuilder was the major figure in Scottish heavy industry, had already taken action. In April 1931, at a special conference of the Convention of Royal Burghs, the Scottish National Development Council was set up by a resolution moved by the Duke of Montrose and seconded by William Power, after an agitation led by David Anderson, editor of the *Daily Record*. It thus had, politically, a pedigree close to that of the Scottish Party. Lithgow then subsidised the SNDC until 1935, when the government undertook this through the newly created Commissioner for the Scottish Special Area.[51] This was an attempt to check any appeal nationalism might have to businessmen, but by invoking government in the drive to industrial diversification and regional 'planning', the SNDC also made industry concern itself with a Scottish community it had not hitherto acknowledged. Its magazine *Scotland* (founded in 1934) was soon running articles by literary nationalists – even by MacDiarmid himself.

In 1935 Collins created the Scottish Economic Committee, theoretically a subcommittee of the SNDC but in fact almost wholly financed by the Scottish Office and the Scottish Commissioner. Its Secretary-General was Sir William Goodchild, a high-flying Anglo-Scottish civil servant; his deputy was a young economist, J. A. A. Porteous, who had just published *The New Unionism* (1935), a manifesto of 'corporatist' economic planning, drawing both on the ideas of J. M. Keynes and those advanced mainly by the dissident Conservatives in Political and Economic Planning, set up in 1935. Shortly afterwards, Collins died, and was succeeded by a politician deeply identified both with 'planning' and with Scottish culture, Walter Elliot. A Glasgow University friend of Osborne Mavor (James Bridie), Elliot was a learned and imaginative man who elaborated Collins' initiatives into a range of state authorities and made the Empire Exhibition of 1938, which was held in Glasgow, the showpiece for new Scottish architecture and design. In 1936 he was also a founder, along with Tom Johnston, of the Saltire Society. This aimed to encourage Scottish culture to emulate the Enlightenment of the eighteenth century, a significant rehabilitation of a period depreciated both by the evangelical Victorians and the 'renaissance men'.[52]

Elliot's various initiatives, further developed by Johnston during World War II, integrated Scottish literature and culture within a bipartisan programme of economic and social development, and in so doing changed its context. This shift from cultural struggle to combating social problems had already been foreshadowed by Edwin Muir's *Scottish Journey* (1935) and by Lewis Grassic Gibbon, both in the 'positivistic' rural-to-urban evolution of his *Scots Quair* trilogy of 1932-34, and his rhetorical rejection of Scottish nationalism in *The Scottish Scene*, which he produced with MacDiarmid in 1934:

> I would welcome the end of Braid Scots and Gaelic, our history, our nationhood under the heels of a Chinese army of occupation if it could cleanse the Glasgow slums.[53]

To MacDiarmid this was 'a purple passage of emotional humanism – the very antithesis of the way those evils can be overcome'.[54]

> I on the other hand would sacrifice a million people any day for an immortal lyric. I am a scientific Socialist. I have no use whatever for emotional humanism.[55]

On the other hand MacDiarmid continued to commit himself to the political struggle through the Communist Party (which regarded him as an ally it could do without and expelled him in 1938), while the emotional 'point of rest' of Gibbon's *Scots Quair* remained, for most of its Scots readers, the central figure, 'Chris Caledonia', rather than her son, the 'scientific Socialist' Ewan Tavendale.

This reorientation was politically more conservative, if socially more radical. It was radical, too, in the means by which it was projected. Elliot supported SNDC's Films of Scotland committee and the making of documentary and feature films in Scotland. In a film-besotted nation the positive national image presented in many films of the 1930s and 1940s, well covered by the press, helped encourage an identity which countered the centralising pressures of the war and the subsequent Labour government. Yet the roots of this involvement lay in Elliot and Johnston's experience of the Empire Marketing Board in the late 1920s, which had given the young

John Grierson his first chance as director.[56] Their Scottish prescriptions were part of the 'imperial federation' tradition, reinforced in the later 1930s by the need to organise on a UK basis against Fascism.

MacDiarmid was not alone in regarding this consensus as itself proto-fascist in its implications, and this line was articulately put forward by an exiled left-wing group with strongly anti-imperialist inclinations, the London Scots Self-Government Committee, headed by Tom Burns and Norrie Fraser and enjoying the support of Naomi Mitchison. Burns' tract *The Real Rulers of Scotland* (1938) alleged the existence of a Scots industrial-political complex, and a further pamphlet attacked the SEC's inquiry into Highland affairs as promising *Fascism for the Highlands*. But ultimately it was pulled apart: its 'popular front' members aligned themselves with Johnston's reforms, and its nationalist element, under the poet and classicist Douglas Young – another of MacDiarmid's disciples – wrested control of the SNP from MacCormick in 1942.[57]

The wartime by-election successes (or near successes) by the SNP and groups sharing its ideals strengthened Johnston's hand.[58] The further impact of MacCormick's Covenant Movement in the late 1940s similarly influenced the Conservatives after 1951. But the international economic climate seemed to show that the prosperity of the years before 1914 had returned, and a cosmetic Scottish identity could be imposed on the same industrially derived scheme of values which had dominated the Scots media before World War I. However, the onset of chronic industrial decline and the loss of control by the Scottish business class, after 1958, was quickly reflected in political behaviour which diverged from the UK norm, and revived the concerns of the 1930s. The Unionist intelligentsia had its last chance in the 1950s, and fumbled it. Elliot might have made something of the Scottish Office, but Churchill chose instead to give it to his chief whip, James Stuart. Stuart's successors were unimpressive, and when Macmillan took his initiatives in the early 1960s, he relied on a Johnstonian publicity apparatus which, if ageing, was also nationalistic.

The publication of George Davie's *Democratic Intellect* in 1961 and MacDiarmid's *Collected Poems* in 1962 coincided with heavy industrial closures on a huge scale and a major expansion in higher education: a degree of disruption rarely encountered in peacetime. Underlying pressures also included the takeover of the bastion of literary Unionism, *The Scotsman*, by Roy Thompson in 1954, the impact of commercial television on another Unionist redoubt, the BBC (which had virtually destroyed every cultural nationalist who had tried to impose his will on it), and the absorption into the Labour movement mainstream, via the unions and CND, of the popular culture revival that the Communist Party had encouraged. By the election of the Wilson government in 1964 the utopianism and solidarity of the orthodox Left was in its decadence, but an intellectual fluidity was perceptible, which mirrored not only the greater economic salience of training and the service industries, but the weakening of sectarian divisions. To go back to Gramsci, the 'organic' was converging with the 'traditional'.

In the introduction to *Lucky Poet* (1942) MacDiarmid revived Carlyle's distinction between 'can-ning' and 'ken-ning'. Technological capability had to be matched by comprehension. In 1928 he had written to R. E. Muirhead that he did not expect the latter to happen for twenty-five years.[59] In fact, the decade after 1958 – with the impact of the 'affluent society', motorisation, television, and contraception – was to pose the same sort of earthquake-like challenge that Carlyle had recognised a century and a half before: a period in which 'no man knows his whereabout'.

In 1968, with the first sustained impact of political nationalism, MacDiarmid's prediction seemed to be borne out, but the learning process since then has been a particularly complicated and frustrating one. The 'kenner' – the speculative and imaginative intellectual – is almost by definition remote from the day-to-day activity of politics, in which mere survival depends on constant success in manoeuvre, and this has consistently registered within the nationalist movement. There are booms, when the intellectuals and journalists convert the momentary boost of – say – a by-election success into a fundamental political alteration. There are also bruises, when the political leadership's goal of consolidation and success in manoeuvre conflicts with the intellectuals' notion of creating movements for wider social change. MacDiarmid's own wayward and frequently disastrous political career dramatised this disjunction, as indeed did the referendum debacle of 1979.

If the longer-term consequence of this setback has been more positive, the recovery of that notion of a Scottish mission to the world with which MacDiarmid ended 'A glass of pure water': 'It is our turn now. The call is to the Celt,' the resulting social philosophy will have to pass muster before the gaze of these severe shades – Cunninghame-Graham, Geddes, Buchan, Elliot, Johnston, MacDiarmid. Its aims – civic, social, ecological – will have to be ambitious enough to comprehend a world situation fraught with more problems and crises than opportunities: a task much more demanding than obtaining *entré* to the club of well-doing European regions.

4

The Impact of 1979 on the SNP

IAN O. BAYNE

1979 was without the shadow of a doubt the most traumatic year in the SNP's fifty-year history. The disappointment and bitterness occasioned by the failure to secure an elected Scottish Assembly – albeit with the limited powers detailed in the Labour government's 1978 Scotland Act – as a result of the constitutionally unprecedented stipulation in the rigged March referendum that it had to obtain the support of at least 40% of the potential electors as well as of a majority of those actually voting left an indelible mark on the party's collective psyche from which it has yet to recover.

The ensuing result in the May election in which the SNP lost nine of its eleven parliamentary seats and saw its share of the Scottish vote slump to 17.3% from its peak general election performance of 30.4% gained at the October 1974 general election did little to restore its already shattered political and psychological health. Instant initial reactions to this election disaster included the suggestion of one prominent defeated SNP candidate that the Scottish electorate had simply 'gone on holiday from the devolution issue',[1] while the party's Labour opponents, themselves disgruntled at the loss of office, rubbed salt in the SNP's gaping wounds by interpreting the result as just punishment for the action of the eleven SNP MPs in voting to bring down the Callaghan administration in the historic Commons debate at the end of March on a Tory 'No Confidence' motion.

This refrain was to be repeated *ad nauseam* for most of the ensuing decade. In hindsight it is easy to admit that the vote against the Labour government may not have been the wisest decision the SNP ever took, and that it might have been more prudent to have abstained on a Tory 'No Confidence' resolution – so as subsequently to avoid any degree of responsibility for ushering in a decade of Thatcherism. At the same time any 'objective' – or at any rate fair-minded – analysis of the total circumstances in which the decision was taken would surely have to conclude that the Labour government had itself 'decisively' lost control of the situation both in Parliament and in 'the country'.

The referendum had been preceded by the 'winter of discontent' in which Labour's 'allies' in the trade union movement had sought to undermine the government's incomes policy. As a consequence Labour's popularity had slumped throughout the United Kingdom, a process from which even its traditional Scottish strongholds had not been altogether immune, and this itself had been a factor in the poor referendum result: especially as Labour propaganda on the 'Yes' or 'pro-devolution' side had actually featured Prime Minister Callaghan's personal support for a Scottish Assembly at a time when he was being successfully portrayed in the media as an incompetent who was insufficiently concerned about the scale and spread of industrial disruption.

In the aftermath of the referendum debacle – which had been partially orchestrated after all by Scots Labour MPs like Norman Buchan and George ('Mister Forty Per Cent') Cunningham, the expatriate Islington MP, who had together been responsible for the inclusion of the referendum provisions in the Scotland Act as well as by Tam Dalyell, the vociferous leader of the Labour 'Vote No' Campaign – the clear priority of the SNP MPs was to do what they could to try and save their seats in the ensuing general election which could not be delayed beyond six months.

Moreover, as most of the eleven SNP MPs represented constituencies which had previously been held by Conservative MPs it was at least dubious if their prospects for re-election would have been genuinely enhanced by any parliamentary action – or inaction – which risked being misinterpreted as merely partisan – as distinct from strategic – support for the failing Labour administration.

To have provided a life-support machine for a Labour government whose own leading participants had already lost the will to govern, as some of them were subsequently to concede,[2] would not have led to the delivery of devolution – which following the 'indecisive' referendum was politically a 'dead duck' despite contrary government posturings about placing it in 'cold storage', the so-called 'Frankenstein solution' – nor would it have magically restored the SNP's already failing electoral credibility.

The previous year, 1978, had been a year of electoral disaster for the party – with three successive parliamentary by-election defeats' – at Garscadden, at Hamilton (despite the candidacy of the 'charismatic' senior vice-chairman Margo MacDonald) and at Berwick and East Lothian, and with a poor performance in the regional elections in which Labour saw off the SNP challenge with almost effortless ease.

In contrast the 1977 district council elections – which occurred in the immediate aftermath of the collapse of the Scotland and Wales Bill, ambushed on a guillotine motion by a coalition of dissident Labour MPs with the Tory opposition assisted by the Liberals – had produced sweeping SNP gains. In retrospect it is perhaps a pity that a 'No Confidence' resolution had not been pushed through Parliament at that time rather than two years later, since the SNP was poised to make substantial parliamentary gains at an ensuing 1977 election: though no doubt for that very reason and because of their hostility to devolution the Tories themselves were reluctant to deliver the necessary knockout blow.

In any event, and for the record, it should be emphasised – especially in view of the subsequent and contrary mythology of the Nationalist Left – that the fateful decision of the eleven SNP MPs to vote against the government in March 1979 – understandably characterised by Prime Minister Callaghan as 'turkeys voting for Christmas' – was taken with the virtually wholehearted support of the party's NEC and rank-and-file membership.

The ground was laid for that decision at the Dundee National Council meeting held on Saturday, 3 March 1979, when the party was in a highly emotional state following the declaration on the previous day of the referendum results throughout Scotland. The results were declared region by region; and one of their most intriguing – and from an SNP standpoint worrying – aspects was that while the populous Labour-dominated regions had managed to return a 'Yes' majority without however overcoming the '40% barrier' in a single instance, both Grampian and Tayside Regions – each with three SNP MPs apiece – had actually voted 'No'.

On my own way to the meeting – which I attended both as a National Council delegate and a prospective parliamentary candidate – I encountered George Reid, the party's 'gradualist' and left-of-centre MP for Clackmannan and East Stirlingshire and a former TV presenter. He forecast that the 'suicide pilots' would be out in force at the day's proceedings, and so it turned out to be: the NEC resolution, proposed by Margo MacDonald, calling on the Parliamentary Group to threaten the government with a general election unless it moved speedily towards the implementation of the Scotland Act, was passed by acclamation.

Even if the MPs had wanted to defy such an overwhelming mandate internal party pressures would have made it impossible for them to do so. An earlier and unsuccessful attempt to bring down the government – at the end of the Queen's Speech debate in the autumn of 1978 – had already uncovered serious divisions between the Parliamentary Group and the NEC on questions of parliamentary and political strategy.

The Parliamentary Group headed by Donald Stewart, MP for the Western Isles since 1970, had decided to vote against the government and in defiance of the NEC – who, fearing the consequences for devolution of a 'premature' Tory victory, had publicly and unsuccessfully pled with the MPs to stay their hand, an approach which probably had the majority backing of the leading activists and prospective parliamentary candidates, including myself, in the constituencies. In the event George Reid had defied the SNP whips to vote the other way and in accordance with the NEC recommendation, while Hamish Watt, the member for Banff, had abstained, and partly as a result the government had survived.

The motivation behind the SNP MPs' majority decision in this instance was clearly concern for their own electoral skins – not an entirely unworthy motivation since, arguably, the party's political credibility was inextricably linked with a continuing high profile at Westminster; and once again in retrospect it is possible to speculate that a government defeat at this juncture rather than four or five months later would actually have improved Scottish prospects of securing a 'Yes' vote in the devolution referendum – which Mrs Thatcher had indicated she would still hold in accordance with the terms of the Scotland Act. In that context it might have been easier to have gathered together under the 'Yes for Scotland' banner those anti-Thatcher forces which were to provide the characteristic mode of Scottish politics for the ensuing decade.

With a general election due in any event by October 1979 at the latest, it was essential that internal tensions on such strategic matters should be contained and that the party should enter the forthcoming election campaign on a united front. For this reason in the immediate aftermath of the referendum debacle the SNP – under the direction of senior vice-chairman Margo MacDonald – launched a 'Scotland Said Yes' campaign in a 'last-ditch' attempt to persuade the ailing Callaghan administration to 'deliver the goods' and implement the Scotland Act despite the embarrassing failure to meet the '40% requirement'.

As the May 1979 election results clearly indicated, in adopting this posture – together with the 'ultimatum' unanimously passed at the Dundee National Council meeting – the SNP had grievously miscalculated the mood of the electorate, who had been demoralised both by the referendum result itself and by adverse social and economic circumstances. Since the end of 1977 Scottish confidence had been progressively undermined by the increased pace of industrial closures and rising unemployment, emotionally reinforced in 1978 by the fiasco of the national football team's performance in the World Cup finals in Argentina.

Against this background the extent of the party's miscalculation can perhaps best be assessed by recalling another telling vignette from those times: the sight of fellow party members jumping up and down in front of TV cameras outside Dundee's Caird Hall, where the crucial post-referendum National Council meeting was being held, incredibly, if somewhat hysterically, shouting, 'We've won! We've won!' is one which remains painfully and indelibly etched on my memory.

The reverses suffered by the SNP at the election a few weeks later at least brought the party down to earth with a resounding bump, though in this respect it is worth bearing in mind that the 17% which it polled nationally on that occasion has yet to be overtaken at any subsequent general election. Yet the party's collective reaction to this election result, coming hard on the heels of the referendum, could be categorised as at best confused and at worst neurotic since it affected different factions and different individuals – and sometimes even the same faction and the same individuals – within the party in different, if occasionally overlapping, ways.

For example, the party's traditionalist or 'fundamentalist' wing uncritically interpreted the result as fair comment on the SNP's 'pro-devolution' stance of the late seventies which allegedly undermined its independence commitment, while ideologically left-wing nationalists equally uncritically embrace the thesis, carefully constructed over the previous decade by our Labour opponents, that it was the decisive verdict on the party's 'right wing' and 'bourgeois-democratic' – or more bluntly 'Tartan Tory' – image.

'Gradualists' contented themselves with the view that the party was paying the price for having been insufficiently alive to the potential of a Scottish Assembly as a 'stepping-stone to independence': a position which could be plausibly countered by the analysis of Labour's pro-devolutionists that it was on the contrary the very identification of the SNP – at a time when its electoral popularity was in any case already declining – with the 'devolutionist' cause which cost Scotland its Assembly.

What was sadly missing from each of these 'total' interpretations was a sense of balance, a sense of proportion. The SNP's relative inexperience prior to 1974 at the centre-stage not just of Scottish but of British politics can perhaps furnish an underlying explanation for the party's curiously counter-productive 'post-1979' behaviour, which can in consequence be seen as a gross over-reaction to the sort of electoral defeat which was not altogether foreign to the party's pre-1974 – or for that matter post-1979 – experience. After all, we would have been quite pleased to have won around 17% of the Scottish vote at the 1970 general election, or even at either or both of the 1983 and 1987 general elections; but in 1979 such a result undoubtedly spelt doom and despondency, if not a cue for the leadership to retire quietly to a private room and put a pistol to its collective head.

For five years of Labour government since 1974 – first under Wilson and then under Callaghan – the SNP's much-maligned eleven MPs, aided and abetted by the narrow party balance in the House of Commons which for most of this time had deprived the government of a guaranteed parliamentary majority, had contrived to keep the issue of Scottish self-government at the top of the Westminster agenda. Their very presence in the House had pressurised the government into making two serious consecutive attempts at introducing devolutionary legislation, the second of which had actually reached the statute book in the form of the Scotland Act – which for all its faults had held out the genuine prospect of an elected Scottish Assembly with limited democratic control over Scottish affairs.

It was therefore undoubtedly galling for all SNP activists to see our new-found capacity to influence the direction of events evaporate in the smoke of the electoral battles of 1979, and to witness the oil-fuelled dreams of a decade disappear to the sound of Establishment gunfire, emanating from both the left and the right of the political spectrum. And it was perhaps especially galling for that highly talented group of young men and women who had gathered round the senor vice-chairman to draw up detailed plans for the implementation of their 'radical' ideals[3] in an independent, or even 'devolved', Scotland in which they had perhaps begun to see themselves wielding ministerial office, to see instead the comprehensive collapse of their lofty ambitions in the space of a few short weeks in the spring and early summer of 1979.

In its initial impact on the SNP the total 1979 experience was tantamount to a death in the family – or even a nervous breakdown. As can happen even in the best families faced with such trying circumstances, existing internal tensions and petty jealousies, coupled with mutual recriminations, rapidly surfaced; and the temptation to seek 'scapegoats' – both in personnel and specific policies and strategies – was inadequately resisted.

THE SNP'S 'SOCIAL-DEMOCRATIC TENDENCY' (1974-1979)

Even before 1979 there was considerable evidence of personality conflict within the party leadership which was compounded by genuine differences of opinion about strategy and about the party's ideological direction. It would be an over-simplified view to represent this running conflict as a clash between the NEC headed by chairman Billy Wolfe and his senior vice-chairman Margo MacDonald, and supported by the full-time headquarters staff, most of whom were the hand-picked protégés of Mrs MacDonald on the one hand, and the eleven SNP MPs, headed by their leader Donald Stewart and effectively reinforced by Mrs Winifred Ewing, the flamboyant victor of the 1967 Hamilton by-election, on the other. But there is sufficient element of truth in this analysis to justify further investigation, though it must be emphasised that it is virtually impossible to disentangle the purely personal from the genuinely political aspects of the emerging conflict, as it developed throughout the latter half of the 1970s.

Not long after the October 1974 election the senior vice-chairman drew the ire of the Parliamentary Group leader by publicly proclaiming that the party was now a 'social-democratic party'. For the vast majority of party members – at least in the industrial belt – this was by no means an outrageous claim, both because it probably reflected their own ideological prejudices and also because it simply 'spelt out' the existing policy profile as outlined in the previous election manifesto.

A particularly strong plank in the party platform for the October election campaign had been provided by a key policy pledge to wage 'war on (Scottish) poverty'. This theme had been developed by George Reid, the ex-Labour Party member sensationally elected in a former Labour stronghold at the February 1974 election; he had produced authentic official statistics to illustrate the relative social and economic deprivation experienced by Scottish working-class people – on all the indicators of multiple urban deprivation the Scots were far worse off than their southern neighbours – and had linked the resolution of this problem of Scottish poverty to a massive cash injection from the oil taxation revenues which would be available to an independent Scotland.

But although this aspect of the party's programme had no doubt been an important factor in the SNP's relative electoral success in October 1974, it had not prevented our Labour opponents from continuing to label us 'Tartan Tories'. This was clearly a cause of considerable concern to the senior vice-chairman and her NEC allies, though it never seems to have occurred to them that in the very process of moving decisively to counteract such a blatant and electorally motivated caricature put out by a clearly rattled Labour Party – by means of adopting a more clearly defined ideological image – they ran the risk of giving it a credibility which it never seriously deserved.

Any examination of the detail of SNP policies long before October 1974 could scarcely have failed to detect a 'left-wing' rather than a 'right-wing' bias, as evident, for example, in the party's long-standing commitment to rid Scotland of all nuclear weapons and in its land policy which in its advocacy of 'repossession' of 'unproductive' land was much more radical than current Labour policy.

The attempt to pin the 'Tartan Tory' label round SNP necks was nevertheless given some degree of academic respectability in the aftermath of the October 1974 election when an alert political scientist[4] noted that only about two of the party's seventy-one parliamentary candidates at the recent election could have been classified as 'working class' according to the Registrar-General's categories. But at a time when in the Labour Party the dominant constituency activists were increasingly being culled from the growing army of professional and public sector employees, this was surely a spurious argument. In 1978 the three successful Labour candidates in three successive Scottish parliamentary by-elections were all middle-class professionals, while today in 1991 this occupational classification would apply to a clear majority of Scotland's forty-nine Labour MPs.[5]

At the same time the party was at a distinct disadvantage in the crucial battle with Labour for working-class votes, especially in the urban-industrial heartlands of West-Central Scotland; not so much because of its policies (of which the public was in any case largely ignorant, a condition which was shared by many party members and which extended moreover to the detail of Labour policies) nor even because of the occupational or class background of SNP candidates as because it simply lacked the Labour Party's strong traditional links with the trade union movement and therefore lacked a power-ful focus for spontaneous working-class loyalty.

The NEC was aware of this defect and had moved to remedy it in 1976 by setting up an 'industrial structure' fronted by a full-time industrial liaison officer – in fact an ex-Labour Party member, Stephen Butler. Constituencies and branches were also encouraged to appoint industrial liaison officers charged with monitoring trade union activity in their branch and constituency areas. In addition an affiliated body, the Association of Scottish National Trade Unionists (ASNTU), initially founded in 1965[6] with Billy Wolfe's encourage-ment, was revived as a means of stimulating SNP members to become actively involved in their own trade unions. Unfortunately its effectiveness was sadly limited for a variety of reasons, including personality conflicts between office-bearers and the NEC as well as the on-going internal argument about strategic direction of which

the trade union dimension was only one aspect, a point which those
who were opposed to a specific SNP involvement in trade union
organisation failed to appreciate.[7]

After all, even the Conservative Party attempted to organise
support within the trade union movement as did the Liberals, so that
support for a trade union dimension within the party's overall
strategy did not necessarily imply approval of an overt 'social-
democratic' – and still less of an overt 'socialist' – orientation. The
adoption of such an ideologically explicit party 'image', as favoured
by most NEC members, was not regarded with any great enthusiasm
by most of the party's MPs: not because they were covert 'Tartan
Tories' but essentially because it seemed to them that it might
prejudice their prospects of re-election in constituencies with large
traditionally Tory – or even 'Liberal' – elements.

It could also be argued that even in West-Central Scotland – where
in October 1974 the SNP had taken second place in twenty-five out
of twenty-eight Labour-held constituencies (and had even captured
Dunbartonshire East, a three-way 'marginal') – the unambiguous
expression of a 'left-wing' bias might effectively alienate 'tactical'
Tory voters without attracting a compensatory element of Labour
voters required for electoral victory.[8] It was at the very least a 'high
risk' strategy, and represented a departure from the strategic formula
which had taken the SNP in October 1974 to within 6% of
overtaking Labour as Scotland's most popular party.

The essence of this formula lay in its built-in capacity for 'flexible
response' which allowed the party's candidates to vary their
campaigning approach in accordance with the political and
economic geography of the various constituencies they were
contesting across the country. Not surprisingly, our increasingly
panic-stricken opponents from both sides of the Labour-Tory divide
castigated this apparent attempt on our part to be 'all things to all
men'. But such criticism seriously misrepresented the SNP's whole
raison d'être – which was not the creation of a 'social-democratic',
and still less of a 'Socialist' or a 'Tory' Scotland, but the creation of
a *democratic, self-governing Scotland*. For this goal to stand a
chance of ever being reached it had long been the perception of the
party's traditional 'old guard' leadership – which had after all been
responsible for masterminding the SNP's remarkable resurgence
through the 1960s to its peak general election performance in
October 1974 – that it would be necessary for the party to maintain
its appeal across as broad a political spectrum as possible.[9] Within
this perspective it seemed particularly inappropriate for the party to
attempt to pre-empt any ideological decisions which properly
belonged to the polical institutions of a free Scotland.

The traditionalists were reinforced in this view by their shrewd observation that contrary to popular mythology the Scottish electorate were not so overwhelmingly pro-Labour as a superficial glance at post-war general election statistics might seem to indicate, in fact the only party to have achieved a majority of the Scottish popular vote had been the Conservative Party, in 1955; while the subsequently prevailing pattern of Labour domination in Scottish parliamentary representation was a back-handed compliment from a Labour standpoint to an unjust electoral system, from which not just the SNP but also the Scottish Liberal Party, and even the Scottish Tories, also suffered through a virtually guaranteed under-representation.

Another factor favouring the maintenance of a 'broad' electoral strategy had been evident in Scottish (and British) politics since the mid-sixties, and consisted of the progressive 'de-alignment' of class and party allegiance.[10] This had been initially signposted by the 'Liberal revival' of the mid-1960s which had led to the election of five Scottish Liberal MPs, and had come to a fuller fruition in the SNP's 1974 successes.

Indeed, in its October 1974 campaign – still today the most successful general election campaign the party has ever fought – the SNP made a deliberate play for the 'de-aligned' – or crypto-social-democratic(?) – vote. One of our campaign songs, adapted from a well-known chart-topper by Simon and Garfunkel, contained the following words:

'I've voted once for Both Sides Now –
For Right and Left, and yet somehow
It's their illusions I recall –
I really don't like them at all.'

But with the election in 1975 of Mrs Thatcher as Conservative leader and the consequential breakdown of the 'Butskellite' consensus which had established the parameters for the main 'two-party' political battle in Britain throughout the post-war period ideological, Left-Right, obsessions once more moved centre-stage, and the demand that the SNP adopt a more precise ideological position within the political spectrum assumed increasing plausibility. The 1979 election result seemed to confirm a suspected decline – not just in Scotland but throughout Britain – in the popularity of 'middle-of-the-road' politics, with Liberals south of the border as well as the SNP losing ground.

On the other hand, the subsequent foundation in 1981 of the SDP, together with the electoral advances made by the new Liberal-SDP alliance at by-elections and at the 1983 general election, were to revive the contrary suspicion that the 1979 obituaries for consensus politics were premature. The 24.5% share of the Scottish vote gained by the Alliance in 1983 represented a 16.2% *increase* over the Liberal share of the vote in October 1974, a figure which, significantly, was less than 3% short of the overall *decline* in the SNP share of the vote throughout the same period.

Back in 1976 it had been the turn of the SNP Parliamentary Group to offend the party's NEC: by voting against the government's Aircraft and Shipbuilding Nationalisation Bill. The MPs' motivation did not lie in a doctrinaire hostility to nationalisation but in a justifiable concern about retaining some degree of Scottish control over the already declining Scottish shipbuilding industry. But the matter was badly handled, with Hamish Watt tactlessly tearing up an STUC telegram calling on the Group to support government subsidies for the industry, and the NEC being left to carry out a damage limitation exercise.

Subsequent relations between the Parliamentary Group and the NEC were not improved by the putative suggestion of the vice-chairman for publicity, Stephen Maxwell, recently elected as a Lothian Regional councillor, that the highly successful 'Scottish oil' campaign which had been pioneered in the early 1970s by the Dundee East MP Gordon Wilson, should be adapted or even quietly dropped as it exposed the party to the charge of 'selfishness': a taunt frequently thrown at the SNP indeed – by Labour activists whose concern for the welfare of the English working class, deprived of a share in the oil-taxation revenues, was unlikely to have been as great as their anxiety to defend their urban-industrial Scottish fiefdoms against the SNP's electoral challenge.

THE 79 GROUP TAKEOVER BID (1979-1983)

Within weeks of the 1979 election open ideological warfare – presaged by such earlier disputes between the NEC and the Parliamentary Group – had broken out in the SNP, with the formation in June of the 79 Group under its initial title of the Interim Committee for Political Discussion.

In boldly stating its ultimate objective as a 'socialist and republican Scotland' the Group went much further ideologically than its leading lights – Margo MacDonald and Stephen Maxwell – had ever dared to go. The party had always hitherto eschewed any formal commitment to republicanism as it was justifiably felt that this would be electorally unattractive and even politically divisive – especially in view of the inevitably sectarian connotations to which it would give rise among Protestant working-class communities in West-Central Scotland. Likewise the novel commitment to full-blooded 'socialism', however vaguely defined,[11] seemed to evoke the sort of militant extremism identified with Trotsyist entryist factions within the Labour Party, or with its 'Bennite' wing.

Such ideological aspirations did not supply the primary motivation for the Group's formation. Its principal short-term aim was simply to alter the party's image in line with the Group's preferred electoral strategy;[12] though unfortunately this was based on a deeply flawed analysis of the 1979 election and referendum results and on an equally flawed set of assumptions about the nature of the traditional Labour vote.

The Group seemed to attribute the decline in the SNP vote almost exclusively to a direct transfer of votes from the SNP to the Labour Party when the truth is that we lost slightly more votes to the Conservatives, whose 1979 share of the Scottish vote increased by 6.7% over its October 1974 performance, than we did to Labour, who only managed a 5.2% increase. As we even lost votes to the 'middle-of-the-road' Scottish Liberal Party whose share of the Scottish vote increased by 0.7%, despite an overall drop of 4.3% in the Liberal share of the UK vote, it was difficult to draw any firm conclusions regarding the relationship between the SNP's decline in popularity and its ideological image: other than that we seemed to be losing significant chunks of support right across the political spectrum.

In its eagerness to propose a solution to the party's undoubted electoral problems the 79 Group chose to ignore this rather obvious point.[13] It seemed as if they were so mesmerised by Labour's continuing success in securing yet again a majority of Scottish parliamentary seats – forty-four out of seventy-one on this occasion, though on only 41.5% of the Scottish vote – that they were quite prepared to encourage the party to risk the permanent alienation of traditional 'Tory' – or even of 'middle-of-the-road' and 'floating' – voters in an all-out bid to supplant Labour as the most popular Scottish party. They totally failed to appreciate that in a political system which is structured to suit the electoral interests of the two major parties it is virtually suicidal for any 'third party' attempting to 'crack the system' to limit its campaigning options in such a hopelessly naïve way.

The Group's analysis of the referendum results was equally un-sophisticated. Simply because Labour-voting regions had returned mainly narrow 'Yes' majorities while 'Tory' and 'Liberal' regions had voted 'No', they too readily concluded that the only support worthy of SNP cultivation was working-class support. This blithely ignored the fact that many middle-class – and even Tory-voting – Scots actually voted 'Yes', while many others were only inhibited from so doing by the skilful anti-Labour (as well as anti-SNP) propaganda of the 'No' campaign.[14]

The other main flaw in the 79 Group strategy – namely that if only the SNP were to appear in its true Socialist colours the working-class vote would fall into its lap – was grounded in the curious assumption that the typical working-class Labour voter is motivated by an idealistic passion for the socialist (or at least radical) reconstruction of Scottish society. Nothing could be further from the truth. The typical Scottish Labour voter is an essentially 'conservative' creature of ingrained electoral habit, dedicated to the defence of what 'he' perceives to be 'his' own class interests, and in this respect bears an uncanny resemblance to the typical middle-class Scottish Conservative voter.

What worries such incorrigible Labour voters about the SNP is not its sociological 'conservatism' – which nowadays it largely shares with the Scottish Labour leadership – but its political, or at any rate constitutional, radicalism. The SNP's 'traditionalist' leadership was only too well aware of this electoral reality, and had therefore long sought to cloak its genuine 'radicalism' in a reassuring veneer of middle-class – and even middle-aged – respectability.

Ironically most 79 Group members were themselves from middle-class professional backgrounds – though, admittedly, also from a younger generation than most other SNP members. They were not therefore particularly well equipped to give the party the sort of sociological 'image' which they imagined would be instantly appealing to traditional Labour voters, though why the latter should in any case feel impelled to transfer their allegiance to a party which looked so similar to the one they were being asked to abandon was never fully explained.

For all its faults the 79 Group could nevertheless have been easily tolerated by the rest of the SNP if it had been content to remain as a mere discussion group organising seminars and conference fringe meetings. It soon became evident that the Group's real purpose was to capture the party's key policy-making processes, and gradually freeze out the more traditionalist – and therefore in their eyes 'ideologically unsound' – elements from the party leadership. Some of the main architects of party policy in the 1970s were among its founder-members: for example, Dr Gavin Kennedy, the economist and former Labour Party member, and Andrew Currie, a party specialist in industrial policy, as well as national office-bearers Margo MacDonald and Stephen Maxwell.

At the postponed 1979 annual conference the 79 Group accordingly made its first bid for control of the party. But in the contest for the party chairmanship, now vacated by Billy Wolfe, Stephen Maxwell was decisively defeated by Gordon Wilson, one of the party's two remaining MPs, while even Margo MacDonald was ousted from her post as senior vice-chairman – which she had held for five years – by the former 'fundamentalist' MP for Aberdeenshire East, Douglas Henderson.

Eighteen months later, at the 1981 Aberdeen conference, the 79 Group's star recruit, Jim Sillars – the former Labour MP whose breakaway Scottish Labour Party was eclipsed by his own election defeat – was elected as the SNP's vice-chairman for policy, and this perhaps marks the high point of the Group's formal influence on SNP affairs. Five of Jim Sillars' new 79 Group colleagues – including Stephen Maxwell – were also elected to serve on the 1981-82 executive, and at Sillars' instigation the party adopted a new commitment to 'civil disobedience' as a strategy for challenging the Thatcher government's continuing lack of a 'Scottish mandate'.

The same conference also supported a resolution which effectively committed the party to a policy of unilateral withdrawal from NATO, thereby placing the SNP on this issue to the left of the Italian Communist Party, though there is some doubt as to whether this can be attributed solely to the influence of the 79 Group, as the SNP has always had a strong 'pacifist' faction.

The subsequent 'civil disobedience' campaign, orchestrated by the new policy vice-chairman, failed to set Scotland even metaphorically alight, though the illegal burglary of the Scottish Assembly building – carried out by Sillars himself together with six 79 Group colleagues – did coincide with an encouraging increase in SNP support – which quickly disappeared in the wake of the increasing popularity, north as well as south of the border, of the recently launched Social Democratic Party. It had been assumed by the 79 Group's gurus that the SDP challenge was totally irrelevant to Scottish politics;[15] but Roy Jenkins' victory in the Glasgow Hillhead by-election in March 1982 – with a strong SNP candidate, George Leslie, coming a poor fourth despite a hard-fought campaign – exposed the inadequacy of this assumption.

The traditionalists' patience was at an end. At the Ayr conference in May leading SNP personalities, including Mrs Winifred Ewing, the party's sole MEP, launched yet another internal group, the Campaign for Nationalism[16] – which was designed to dissociate the party from a narrow class-based electoral strategy and to reassert a broad-based 'national' strategy. This anti-79 Group stratagem worked since a frustrated party chairman threatened resignation if his emergency resolution banning all internal groups was not immediately passed.

But Gordon Wilson's decisive action was merely the signal for an intensification of the internal battle for party control between its 'Left' and traditionalist wings. The 79 Group was given three months to disband; with great reluctance it agreed to comply, while simultaneously electing a committee to establish a new – and ostensibly cross-party – 79 Group Scottish Socialist Society. The NEC reacted by expelling the committee members, including Stephen Maxwell and Alec Salmond, the future MP and Party leader; but after successive stormy National Council meetings this 'sentence' was commuted to a six-month 'suspension' ending just in time to allow the 'dissidents' to participate in the 1983 general election campaign.[17]

'MODERATE, LEFT-OF-CENTRE' FUNDAMENTALISM – 1983-199?

But the party apparently paid a heavy electoral price for the prolonged public feuding. Its 1983 share of the Scottish vote plummeted by as much as one-third from its 1979 level – to a mere 11.7%, less than 0.5% higher than its percentage share back in 1970; and while it retained its two parliamentary seats it lost fifty-three deposits.

The relative popularity of the new Liberal-SDP Alliance, which attracted nearly 25% of the Scottish vote and secured the election of eight Scottish MPs, was an additional and possibly even more significant factor contributing to the escalating SNP decline.

In the ensuing years at least the public feuding has virtually ended, and a pragmatic 'unholy' alliance has been formed at the top of the party between the formerly warring factions. Two of the 1982 'expellees', Alec Salmond and Kenny MacAskill, later served as national office-bearers alongside their former 79 Group colleague Jim Sillars and in apparent harmony with the restyled 'national convener' Gordon Wilson and with party president Winifred Ewing. Salmond indeed has since succeeded to the leadership following Wilson's resignation at the 1990 conference.

In addition the SNP has at last acknowledged its dominant 'social-democratic' ideological tendency, and officially describes itself as a 'moderate, left-of-centre party', though some of the policies and strategies it has since espoused more properly belong to the more militant tradition of the far left.

In particular the wholehearted support which the party gave to the 1984-85 miners' strike, led by the NUM President Arthur Scargill in apparent breach of Rule 43 of his own union's constitution, did little to improve the SNP's credibility with genuinely 'moderate, left-of-centre' voters: especially at a time when Neil Kinnock, the Labour leader, was frantically distancing himself from the miners' picket-line behaviour, and did even less to ensure the survival of the Scottish coalfields.

The 1987 election nevertheless produced a slight 2.3% increase over the party's 1983 share of the Scottish vote, and the SNP also won back three rural seats lost to the Tories in 1979. It simultaneously lost its two existing seats, including Gordon Wilson's urban-industrial Dundee East constituency to Labour, which enjoyed its best post-war general election in Scotland, winning fifty seats out of seventy-two – admittedly on only 42.4% of the vote – and stretching its 'lead' over the SNP from 23.4% in 1983 to 28%.

Yet despite this clear evidence[18] that the type of electoral strategy recommended by the Nationalist Left was not reaping electoral dividends,[19] the party's policy vice-convener, Kenny MacAskill, soon began laying plans for a 'poll-tax non-payment campaign' – aimed above all at disgruntled Labour voters. This campaign has apparently enjoyed only limited success even among the party's committed supporters,[20] despite the fact that Donald Dewar, the 'moderate left-of-centre' Scottish Labour leader, steadfastly resisted pressure from his own ranks to launch a similar non-payment campaign.

Even at the 1988 Govan by-election the BBC 'exit polls' indicated that the SNP's poll-tax policy was not a significant factor in Jim Sillars' 'famous victory': which could be attributed to a variety of other factors including the candidate's outstanding personal qualities and unrivalled political experience as well as his strong 'anti-Thatcher' credentials. Moreover, the recent dumping of the 'non-payment campaign' – despite MacAskill's protests, suggests that the Salmond leadership has realised the limitations of this campaigning weapon.

Two other major policy initiatives have been taken by the SNP leadership since 1983. First, at the 1984 conference the party chairman's long-cherished notion of a directly elected Scottish Constitutional Convention as a mechanism for the delivery of self-government – which he had unsuccessfully introduced into the Commons in a 1980 Private Member's Bill – was adopted as official SNP policy; and second, at the 1988 conference Jim Sillars persuaded the party to support his idea of 'Independence in Europe'. In each of these policy initiatives the SNP to its great credit moved decisively away from the 'separatist' image with which it was saddled, however unfairly, in the 1970s. Both steps were taken as a result of a pragmatic recognition of present-day political realities both in the EC in the light of the 1992 approach of closer integration and in Scotland itself – where the people are not yet ready (and might never be ready) to sever all economic and political ties with the rest of the United Kingdom.

Back in the 1970s the 'fundamentalists' had put up a strong rearguard action against the NEC's essentially 'gradualist' pro-devolution strategy, and in the disillusioned aftermath of the 1979 election they had easily secured the party's overwhelming support –

at its postponed annual conference – for a 'hardline' resolution calling for 'no more dealings in assemblies, devolution or meaningful talks'. But by the mid-eighties they seemed to be once again in retreat.

In the longer historical perspective these constantly recurring debates on the constitutional issue at the heart of the SNP's concern – which can be traced back to the party's 1928-34 origins – are probably more significant than the 'Left-Right' arguments which in the past decade have attracted greater publicity. The internal conflict on the 'fundamentalist v. gradualist' question does not provide a mirror-image of the ideological split, and strange bedfellows are frequently to be found on either side of the argument. In recent years nevertheless, most prominent SNP left-wingers have tended to line up behind the 'gradualist' position.

Unfortunately this ostensible 'moderation' has too often been obscured by the SNP Left's own brand of ideological 'fundamentalism' on both policy and strategic issues. In January 1989 the SNP walk-out from the cross-party talks to establish the Constitutional Convention even seemed to indicate that there was little to choose between such left-wing 'fundamentalism' – now apparently being extended to the constitutional issue – and the traditional 'fundamentalism' of the 'social-democratic Right'.

Both 'wings' of the party were at any rate represented in the delegation – which consisted of national convener Gordon Wilson, Parliamentary Group leader Margaret Ewing, and the Govan victor, Jim Sillars himself. And its 'withdrawal' decision certainly illustrated that the old 'fundamentalist' skeleton was still capable of rattling away merrily in the SNP family vaults – to the evident consternation of the broad cross-party consensus which the Campaign for a Scottish Assembly had painfully stitched together since its 1980 inception.

Almost as painful as the 'withdrawal' decision itself was the way in which it was taken. Both the NEC and National Council were effectively 'bounced' into ratifying their high-powered delegation's initial decision – since not to have done so would have been interpreted as a vote of no confidence in the party leadership, clearly an inconceivable outcome in the aftermath of the Govan by-election. This was doubtless a factor influencing the delegation's calculations, and it reflects adversely on the patronising attitudes of the SNP hierarchy towards the rank-and-file party membership.

Clearly, ordinary SNP members are not to be trusted with matters of 'high policy' and therefore conference and National Council debates must be stage-managed so as to minimise the possibility of a platform defeat. In opposing the withdrawal from the Constitutional

Convention – which was already a *fait accompli* – at the March 1989 National Council meeting, Isobel Lindsay simply appeared, as she herself said, 'in the role of Frank Bruno'.[21]

Apart from the fact that such arrogance and élitism does not augur well for an independent Scotland's prospects under an SNP government, it seemed particularly inappropriate in view of the limited concrete progress the party has actually made towards that goal – especially over the past decade. Despite the Govan by-election and some good local election results, the party's current electoral strategies, as devised by the now left-dominated NEC, have not exactly been an unqualified success.[22]

At the same time – and paradoxically – the climate of Scottish public opinion has rarely been more favourable to the articulation of a Scottish political identity. Opinion polls in the late 1980s have consistently shown a level of support for 'independence', which at around 30% was running well ahead of the average monthly or yearly support for the SNP: whereas in the 1970s virtually the exact opposite had occurred, and the level of support for 'independence' had consistently lagged behind the level of SNP support by a similar proportion. In addition the Scottish majority for some form of self-government has been consistently higher than it was in 1979.[23]

Yet the party has conspicuously failed to translate this growing support for its fundamental objective into equivalent ballot-box success. It has also failed to grasp that in such circumstances the electoral arithmetic conclusively points to a strategy of cross-party co-operation as a means of achieving self-government: not only because of the 'pro-Assembly' Scottish majority, but also because in three successive general elections Scotland has voted in a decisively different direction from England.

Whatever nice calculations might quite properly concern the party in its internal disputes about ideological orientation, there can be no doubting the overall Scottish 'anti-Tory' majority,[24] which sadly lacks the political focus and the political voice which an Assembly would indisputably bring. And whatever doubts the SNP might justifiably entertain regarding the sincerity of Labour and SLD politicians on the devolution issue, the reality is that without some minimal degree of co-operation from them our own dreams of 'independence' are likely to remain forever confined to the realms of fantasy.

The 1979 experience exposed a variety of ideological and strategic divisions within the SNP which gave rise to a period of bitter internal feuding, and this in turn culminated in the party's worst general election result for over a decade. Since 1983 the NEC has been relatively successful in maintaining a façade of external conformity, though only at the price of increasing left-wing domination which is unrepresentative of the party's wider support. Despite 'gradualist' gestures towards devolution and the 'Scotland in Europe' idea, the 'fundamentalists' have come out of the closet to applaud the decision to withdraw from the Constitutional Convention. The real danger facing the party as it enters the 1990s – which could otherwise be a decade of real political opportunity – is that the price of internal unity could be increasing external irrelevance.

The confusion and disillusionment which threatened to engulf the SNP in 1979 has lingered on throughout the intervening years to distract the party's attention from the very real, if ultimately unquantifiable, growth in Scottish cultural and political conscious-ness that had undoubtedly materialised by the outset of the century's final decade. This has been evident in a number of ways: in the burgeoning self-confidence of the Scottish literary and artistic community, in the expansion of both academic and popular interest in modern (as well as traditional) Scottish history, in the remarkable resilience of Scotland's major financial institutions in the face of external predators and in a difficult commercial climate, and even perhaps in the incredible resurgence of Glasgow as a European city of culture against a backdrop of continuing industrial decline.

In addition the steady expansion of public support for a Scottish political dimension, discreetly fostered by the all-party Campaign for a Scottish Assembly and duly reflected, as already noted, in the public opinion polls, has been impressively solid, and has conspicu-ously failed to track fluctuations in SNP support. Under the impact of the 1979 trauma the party has been unable to capitalise on this situation. Instead it has boxed itself into a sectarian strategy, predicated on an ill-considered contempt for any constitutional initiative which falls short of its own lofty ideal of 'independence nothing less'. This has inevitably inhibited co-operation with other broadly 'nationalist' groups such as the Scottish Labour Action Group.

The alleged transformation of the SNP in the 1980s from a naïve and romantic 'movement' into a hard-headed and left-wing political party has attracted much favourable media coverage, though ironic-ally this has been accompanied by a marked decline in the party's consistently sustained level of support relative to its position in the mid-seventies. Perhaps the party, having made its point regarding its underlying left-wing sympathies and credentials, should now shift its campaigning emphasis back to being a 'movement' once again: since only a broad-based 'national' strategy rather than a relatively narrow, class-based approach can hope to succeed in the central SNP task of constructing a genuinely democratic Scottish polity which is capable of accommodating and containing internal partisan conflict. Within this perspective the party's key role is to facilitate the process of constitutional change and not to provide a detailed paradigm of how it could operate in practice. Above all the electorate ought surely to be discouraged from assuming that support for 'independence' necessarily implies support for a future SNP government.

In his 1955 autobiography[25] John MacCormick made the confident prediction that 'long before the end of this century' a Scottish Parliament would once again be sitting in Edinburgh. The time is running out for the fulfilment of his dream; but if the SNP is to stand a chance of making it before the onset of the next millennium it must first put the agonies of the past decade behind it, and then frankly recognise that we will not be able to do it alone. Only in co-operation with our fellow-Scots, 'from all parties and none',[26] and perhaps through the mechanism of the Constitutional Convention, recalled and reconstituted if necessary after the next election, can we hope in the foreseeable future to make our contribution to the achievement of at least a measure of genuine national self-determination.

5

The Lessons of Ireland for the SNP

BOB PURDIE

> With sleekit Presbyterian moderation the Scots have restrained themselves until it is abundantly clear that the English would be incapable of stopping an insurrection on the Isle of Wight. The Irish had to fight the Black and Tans. The *London Times* has already half surrendered to the Scots. (Tom Nairn, 'Scotland the Three Dreams', *New Left Review*, May-June 1968.)·

Scotland and Ireland have much in common: they are geographically close and have intimate ties of ethnicity, history and culture. The Irish experience, therefore, contains important lessons which can be learned by Scots. It may seem surprising that there has been very little cross-fertilisation between nationalist movements in the two countries, but there are good reasons why this should have been so. There was, for example, the barrier of Ireland's Catholicism and Scotland's Calvinism, and there was a different rhythm of development which meant that while one was reaching a peak, the other was in retreat. In the 1918-21 period, when twenty-six counties of Ireland were being wrested from Westminster control, the Home Rule traditions of Scottish Labour were being supplanted by the idea of reform from Westminster. Although in more recent times the upsurge of Republicanism in Northern Ireland has coincided with a revival of nationalism in Scotland, the fear of sectarian violence spilling over into Scotland has meant that only a fringe element of the Nationalist Left has been prepared to espouse the idea that Ireland offers a model for Scotland.

The roots of the Irish problem lay in the Act of Union of 1800. Like the Scottish Union it was meant to be an incorporative union in which the identity of Ireland would be submerged in a new United Kingdom. The enterprise was flawed from the start because Pitt had meant it to include Catholic Emancipation, but the King blocked such a concession. Thereafter no reform specifically suited to Irish needs could be carried through if it created a precedent which might hurt the landed interest in Britain. Ireland's problems were, as Disraeli put it, that:

a dense population in extreme distress inhabits an island where there is an established church which is not their church and a territorial aristocracy the richest of whom live in distant capitals. Thus you have a starving population, an absentee aristocracy, and an alien Church and in addition the weakest executive in the world. That is the Irish question.[1]

As an agrarian Catholic country in an industrialised Protestant Union, Ireland needed radical reform of land ownership and of the religious establishment, but the landed interest in Britain blocked all effective reforms until the issue became self-government. Then a coalition of Ulster Unionists, old Tories and Liberal imperialists blocked self-government until the issue became insurrection. When policies suited to Irish needs were, with difficulty, forced through the Westminster Parliament, they were usually too little and too late, and often tied to coercive measures. Ireland was never incorporated because the narrow circle of the powerful who controlled British politics refused to rule Ireland according to Irish needs.

For Scotland in contrast, the Westminster Parliament worked imperfectly, but adequately, until the early twentieth century, but it failed Ireland continuously and systematically until 1920; and it has gone on failing Northern Ireland until the present day. If the narrowly based, Anglo-centric, power élite which dominated Westminster did not treat Scotland like Ireland, it was not out of a greater consideration. Scotland's discontents, however, were different from those of the Irish and this is one of the reasons why it is difficult to compare the two nationalist movements.

It is more than a proximity, however, which has linked the fates of Scotland and Ireland. During the latter half of the nineteenth century the Scots/Irish population was an important factor in Scottish politics because it delivered a large, highly disciplined vote to the party favoured by the Irish nationalist leadership – usually the Liberals. But the Irish themselves were insulated from the politics of the country they lived in; it was only with the Irish Treaty in 1921 that they were released from their obligation to subordinate their political aspirations in Scotland, allowing them to participate fully in Scottish politics. When they did, it was to support the Labour Party, who at this time still gave nominal support to Scottish Home Rule; but that was not why the Irish supported it. When the party swung round to Westminster centralism, Irish support, if anything, intensified.

The simple fact of sharing a status as subordinate nations did not mean that there was an automatic strategic or tactical consonance between Irish and Scottish nationalism. Scottish and Irish radical nationalists could be sharply aware of this. In 1889 when Parnell visited Edinburgh shortly after his personal triumph at *The Times* Tribunal, he was greeted by a mass rally of supporters. One organisation, however, inserted a note of criticism into the official booklet of fulsome greetings.

> The Scottish Land Restoration League feels that it is indebted to you for putting Michael Davitt's glorious doctrines well forward in your political action. . . . In later times, induced by your party politics and the idea of obtaining Home Rule from one or other of the two great parties . . . you gave our 'Social Reform' some serious and most ungrateful blows. We hold that it was an error even in your party politics. It was the Democracy that compelled the Liberal Party to take a wise relation to Ireland. It is the Democracy that will compel the full measure of your just demand. But we are aware that this will not be so apparent to you as it would be to a more democratic leader; therefore we have no fault to find with these acts of ours which were injurious to Scottish Land Restoration and Scottish Home Rule. As men of principle we help all reformers whether they help us or no. . . .[2]

One of the signatories, the vice-chairman of the SLRL, John Ferguson, is an example of the difficulty of navigating the cross-currents of Scottish and Irish politics. He was active in Irish exile politics in Glasgow from 1860 onwards. A disciple of J. S. Mill and Henry George, he was a founding member of the Scottish Labour Party in 1888. But his association with Keir Hardie did not last long, and he was expelled for publicly supporting the Liberal Party. In any case, he was not a typical Irish nationalist; a Belfast-born Presbyterian, he was really a radical who pursued reform through Irish Home Rule, the Irish Land League, the Scottish Land Restoration League, the Liberal Party, and the Scottish Labour Party.[3]

Other examples show the marginal nature of such links. During the War of Independence the magazine *Red Hand*, which was published jointly in Glasgow and Belfast, began to break down some of the barriers. Amongst its contributors was the radical Scottish Nationalist Erskine of Mar, who was to influence John MacLean, and it was the most pro-Labour of the Irish nationalist journals.[4] But its influence was largely confined to Ulster, the region of Ireland least affected by the war and where militant Republicanism was weakest.

As for the influence of Ireland on the Scots, Hugh MacDiarmid was inspired to become a nationalist by the 1916 Rising, but it is to the exile James Joyce, not the martyr Padraig Pearse, that we must look in order to explain his poetry. Wendy Wood became a nationalist after meeting Roger Casement's brother Tom in Basutoland in 1913, and during the 1930s she visited Dublin at the invitation of the Republican Women's Organisation, Cuman na mBan.[5] She returned full of enthusiasm, but her writings show only a superficial knowledge of Ireland, and no consistent interest or involvement. In 1934 a delegation of Scottish nationalists visited Dublin as part of a tour of Celtic countries, to examine Irish self-government. They came back praising de Valera, but the Southern Irish state has never been an inspiration for Scots: its inability to hold on to its own people and the confessional influences over the state, as evidence by the Eucharistic Congress in 1932 and the de Valera Constitution, were difficult for most Scots to swallow.

Others have been more concerned *not* to follow the example of Ireland. Tom Johnston warned in 1922 that refusal of Home Rule would 'play into the hands of the extremists' and lead people to 'emulate the example of the people of the sister isle'.[6] The founder of the SNP, Dr John MacCormick, criticised those in the Scottish national movement who 'seemed . . . to look at Scotland through green spectacles and despite a complete lack of historical parallel to identify the Irish struggle with their own'.[7] His speech to the conference which split the National Party of Scotland in October 1933, a statement of his own moderate and pragmatic politics, contained an implicit critique of Irish nationalism:

> We in this hall, I suggested, were not the Scottish nation. . . . The nation was not an abstraction, an imaginary Dark Rosaleen, but a living reality composed of millions of living individual people. It was with the people we had to contend and it was their mood we must seek to interpret. We could only be effective leaders of opinion so long as we did not race too far ahead of those whom we wished to follow us.[8]

MacCormick was dissociating himself from the nationalism which then prevailed in Ireland. Irish nationalists can be divided into two distinct traditions, political and cultural. Political nationalists:

> were men long immersed in British political and cultural life, secularist in their outlook and who admired its liberal democratic ideals . . . they had no sense of Ireland as a separate civilisation, but rather wished that an Ireland modelled on English liberal lines be given its proper status as a partner in the British Imperial mission.[9]

The cultural nationalists, on the other hand:

> Perceiving the nation in *organic* terms . . . portrayed Ireland as a living personality – Cathleen Ni Houlihan – whose individu-

ality had to be cherished in all its manifestations. Revivalism took on the characteristics of a religious movement in which Irish names, language, literature, sports and manufactures were to be adopted and their English equivalents renounced. Its goal was the 'inner' regeneration of a spontaneously evolving decentralised community led by an élite of public-spirited men and women.[10]

This current can be traced back to its intellectual origins in the Romantic movement of nineteenth-century Europe. Romanticism has Scottish origins; it found its initial inspiration in MacPherson's *Ossian* and the writing of Sir Walter Scott. It stressed the individuality of nations, to be found in their history and ethnic cultures; nation-building was the work of clearing the ground of external domination and influence, so that the nation could be itself again. It was introduced to Ireland by the Young Ireland movement in the 1840s, and triumphed over political nationalism when Sinn Féin ousted the Irish Home Rule Party in 1918.

Young Irelanders, like Thomas Davis and James Clarence Mangan, were deeply concerned for the people of Ireland, recognising in them the living receptacles of the Irishness which had to be preserved and fostered. But many who came after saw Irishness as an abstraction to which human beings had to conform, rather than as material which people must rework for themselves in order to express their own individuality. Like all collectivist ideologies, Romantic nationalism could become repressive when broad generalisations were turned into unvarying prescriptions.

The implications are shown in the following extract from a story by James Plunkett:

> 'Farrel hadn't time,' he announced pleasantly . . . 'If it was an English penny dreadful about Public Schools or London crime you'd have time to read it quick enough, but when it's about the poor hunted martyrs and felons of your own unfortunate country by a patriot like Davis you've no time for it. You've the makings of a fine little Britisher. . . . Hold out your hand. If I can't preach respect for the patriot dead into you . . . I'll beat respect into you. Hand.'[11]

It was this attitude which led to the Irish language being turned into an instrument of oppression for those who had no immediate facility for learning it, rather than as a source of joy for those who were able to approach its beauties for themselves. For too many Irish nationalists, Irish culture was seen as a means of purging the country of alien influences, rather than as a way in which Ireland could make a unique contribution to human culture. The attitude was summed up in the programme for a South Armagh Aeridheacht (open air cultural festival) in 1952, which referred to Irish dancing as, 'a bulwark to the imported polkas, tangos and immoral jitterbugging, so common in our ballrooms . . .'.[12]

Scottish nationalism has not completely avoided similar defects, but in Scotland political nationalism was not eclipsed by cultural nationalism. Romanticism did not prosper in the land of its birth; one reason was given by Owen Dudley Edwards:

> . . . those who built their nationalism on the basis of what Scott wrote might readily end up believing what Scott believed: that the past had been a sad business, and they . . . had done their bit to right matters, but there was no point in prolonging old fights and the country was working out well without any further need for radical change.[13]

Nationalism did not become a distinct political movement in Scotland until the 1920s; until that time it had been part of Liberalism and Labourism and it continued to share their common roots in the radical tradition of the eighteenth century. It is rooted in the Enlightenment, rather than in Romanticism. This tradition is epitomised in the poetry of Robert Burns. In the Burnsian tradition the worthy poor are exalted over the worthless rich, the pride of personal achievement over the tinsel show of hereditary privilege and the brotherhood of man and sisterhood of woman over the grasping selfishness of the powerful.

It is most clearly expressed in what appears at first to be one of Burns's most conservative poems, *The Cottars Saturday Night*. The warmth of the peasant family life which he describes is accompanied by a strict patriarchal hierarchy and the youngsters, returning from the farms where they are in service, are instructed to 'mind your duty, duly, morn and night'. Finally they join in worship and:

> . . .kneeling down to Heaven's Eternal King,
> The saint the father and the husband prays:

But Burns is not describing submissive piety:

> Compar'd with this, how poor Religion's pride,
>   In all the pomp of method and of art:
> When men display to congregations wide
>   Devotion's every grace, except the heart!

Burns turns the very conservatism of the peasant family into a triumphant affirmation of the worth of ordinary people:

> From scenes like these, old Scotia's grandeur springs,
>   That makes her Lov'd at home, rever'd abroad:
> Princes and Lords are but the breath of kings,
>   'An honest man's the noblest work of God.'

Burns was to return to this idea in his best-known radical poem,
A Man's a Man For A' That:

> A prince can mak a belted knight,
>   A marquis, duke and a' that:
> But an honest man's *aboon* his might,
>   Gude faith, he *mauna fa'* that.

A Man's a Man is a stirring affirmation of radical principles, but
The Cottars Saturday Night is profoundly Scottish and it provides an
insight into Scottish national sentiment. There is a close analogy to
the relationship with England. South of the border was a nation
which was rich, powerful, haughty and arrogant; north of it a nation
supping hamely fare and wearing hodden grey, but with a quiet sense
of a long history. An educated and cultured people with a rational
and unpretentious religion and a contribution to science and
philosophy far out of proportion to their numbers.

It also gave a sharp sense of distinction within Scotland. There was a
fifth column of privilege within the nation: the landed aristocracy
which had cleared the Highlands of its people, the gentry who made a
comfortable living kowtowing to the English overlords, the clergy who
preferred the Anglican principle of patronage to the right of a
congregation to call its own minister, the coal owners and industrialists
who paid more attention to the City of London than to the welfare of
those who created their wealth. The fact that a good proportion of these
privileged folk spoke in accents indistinguishable from those of the
Southern overlords underlined the point. And didn't Burns tell us that
the Scottish Parliament was 'bought and sold for English gold' by a
'parcel of rogues' who were members of the Scottish nation?

In the early part of the twentieth century the strands of radicalism
and nationalism were combined with socialism to create a distinctive Scottish Labourism.[14] By the 1920s, however, the decline of the
Liberal Party and the drift of the Labour Party towards Westminster-
based centralism gave rise to a separate political nationalist movement. But it carried with it an inheritance from Whiggery,
Radicalism, Liberalism and Labourism. It is true that Irish nationalism influenced some fringe elements, but for most of its history the
national movement in Scotland has been distinctly agnostic about
the principle of separatism and has been willing to work for self-
government within the United Kingdom.

The explanation may be found in a difference between Irish and
Scottish senses of nationhood. Here a tiny difference indicates a
major distinction. Scots refer to 'the Borders'. It is a region with two
sides; the name indicates a relationship not a barrier. The Irish,
however, speak of 'the Border'. For Irish nationalists it is something
which lies across their territory, 'dismembering', 'dissecting' and

'mutilating' it. For Ulster Loyalists it is a bulwark, a dyke against the threat of Catholic domination. But in Scotland the line itself is not disputed, only the political structures which straddle it. This gives us a link to an important lesson to be learned from Ireland.

Because Ireland was predominantly rural, Irish nationalism reflected the attitudes and aspirations of the countryside. And because the Catholic faith was seen as the most distinctive mark of Irish cultural identity, it was deeply and tenaciously Catholic. But this created a problem; not all of Ireland was rural and Catholic. In the north-east there was an industrial society which was predominantly Protestant. The more Irish nationalism asserted its claims and identity, the more Ulster Protestants asserted a British identity. The partition of Ireland has to be seen as a response to this, and to the fact that after independence the southern state reinforced all of the aspects of its state and society which Ulster Protestants found most repugnant.

One result of partition was that, in the mid-twentieth century, Irish nationalism became sidelined by a campaign for territorial unity which ignored both the external power relationships of Ireland and the internal realities of Ireland itself. The All Party Anti-Partition Conference in Dublin's Mansion House in 1950 united nationalists North and South and in all the countries of Irish emigration. There has seldom been a political campaign which was more successful in mobilising its chosen political constituency and in the sophistication of its propaganda. There are also few examples of a political campaign which achieved such meagre results. Almost its only measurable achievement was to polarise the Northern Ireland electorate, giving the Unionists a sweeping victory in the Stormont general election of 1951, and seriously damaging the Northern Ireland Labour Party. The campaign led C. Northcote Parkinson to formulate one of his famous laws: 'Propaganda begins and ends at home'.[15]

The Anti-Partitionists made two fundamental mistakes. The first was to imagine that the British government could be cajoled or pressurised into transferring sovereignty over Northern Ireland to Dublin. The campaign came at the apogee of British nationalism, which was still basking in the pride of its defeat of Nazi Germany, and when Dublin still bore the stigma of wartime neutrality. The war had shown that the southern Irish ports were not essential to British defence, but that those of Northern Ireland had been. Nevertheless Seán MacBride, Foreign Minister in the coalition government of 1948-51, thought it possible to get sovereignty over the North in exchange for Irish membership of NATO. This showed a drastic failure to understand Ireland's place in the new world order and the insignificance of the Northern Ireland problem in the context of the Cold War.[16]

The second mistake was to assume that the dispute was about territory and not about people. Almost none of the reams of books, pamphlets, articles and leaflets produced by the Anti-Partition campaign addressed the Northern Ireland Protestants.[17] It was not considered important to seek to win their consent, and no thought was given as to how Dublin could rule the North without it. Even the Northern Ireland nationalists were elided. By 1955 they were pressing for representation in Dáil Éireann, only to be turned away empty-handed. The frustration caused by the fruitless outcome of the campaign led some of those mobilised by it to take up the gun, with tragic consequences for Northern Ireland today.[18]

Scotland is fortunate in having one of the clearest and least disputed borders in the world. The Scottish sense of identity, therefore, is fairly simple. We are Scots because we are on the other side of the line at which England stops. It is easier to create a sense of Scottishness which does not rely on ethnicity and/or language because the identity of the nation is not in question, only the location of its government. Scots cannot claim any moral superiority for this, but they should be aware of the problems which the dispute about the border created for Irish nationalism.

The insularity of the Anti-Partitionists was not simply a consequence of Ireland's isolation during the Second World War. It was consistent with a particular sense of Irish nationality. Ireland was defined by itself: Irishness was innate and could not be understood by reference to anything outside. England was an incubus, a parasitical and alien attachment which had to be shaken off, not a point of comparision. Scottish nationalism is less insular, because Scottish nationality is much more reliant on a comparison with the large nation across the border; but here there is a danger. If Scotland reclaimed its sovereignty it might not be sufficiently aware of the internal realities of Scotland. Once England ceases to be the main point of comparison for all Scots, the differences and divergences within Scotland will become more apparent.

At present Scotland derives coherence and unity from the fact that, as a nation, it suffers from Westminster policies which tend to concentrate wealth and power in the south east of England. Once a government is established in Scotland it will be distributing such advantages, and incipient rivalries and conflicts of interest may emerge. This was already evident during the run-up to the devolution referendum. Conflicts between the universities and the Scottish Education Department, between the islands and the mainland, between Highlands and Lowlands, between East and West, result in lobbying and jockeying to have particular interests catered for. Within the Labour Party and the SNP serious tactical divisions and differences of principle opened up. Sectarian divisions were not exacerbated, but there was a distinct Protestant-Catholic divide, with the latter tending to prefer to put their trust in Westminster rather than in their Protestant compatriots.

These divisions diluted and weakened the broad national movement within Scotland, and made an already difficult political problem even more difficult. Only by recognising that unity within Scotland is produced by the present relationship with England, and that it cannot be assumed that it will survive a changed set of relationships, can the necessary negotiation and agreement be carried through, so as to maintain unity. The Central Lowlands are still too insular about other parts of Scotland and they often reproduce in miniature the prejudice about the periphery which they complain that they suffer from England. As Ian McCormack of the *West Highland Free Press* puts it:

> What do the readers of the great Scottish dailies hear about the Highlands? 'Sabbath Ferry Row', 'Sit-Down Protest as Wee Free Minister is Carried From the Jetty' . . . If the people of the Lowlands of Scotland don't know what's going on a couple of hundred miles to the north, is it really any wonder that the poll-tax came as a surprise to our neighbours south of Hadrian's Wall?[19]

Had the national movement in Scotland been more aware of Irish experience, the debilitating and divisive debate over the 'West Lothian Question' in the 1970s might have been avoided. The problem of Scottish MPs voting on matters for England which had been devolved to Edinburgh was an entirely foreseeable defect in the devolution legislation; a similar anomaly operated throughout the history of the Northern Ireland Parliament. In fact Harold Wilson himself drew attention to it in 1966, when he attacked the voting record of Unionist MPs in the Commons during the time of his wafer-thin majority following the 1964 general election. He pointed out that 'there have been cases . . . when a government could have fallen with a Northern Ireland vote on Rachmanism in London, although nothing could be said about housing conditions in Belfast'.[20]

Nothern Ireland devolution was deeply flawed. The Stormont Parliament was a sort of Toy Town Westminster, complete with Mace, bewigged Speaker and black-stockinged flunkeys. It adopted the Westminster model of confrontation between Government and Opposition and, by abolishing the proportional representation voting system, it ensured that the Parliament would always be dominated by sectarian blocs; and therefore that it would always maintain a Unionist government. At the same time it had no financial independence, but was reliant on block grants from the British

Exchequer. The central problem was built into the new structure
right from the start. As J. P. Mackintosh pointed out:

> The three Home Rule Bills and the Government of Ireland Act
> were based on a few, relatively simple assumptions and they
> encountered the same intractable problems even at the early
> stage of passage through Parliament. The first assumption was
> that certain 'Imperial' functions could be isolated and left with
> the Westminster Parliament while 'internal matters' could be
> transferred to Dublin or Belfast. This was a more sensible idea
> eighty years ago, when there was not the vast range of
> government activity that there is today, but even in 1886 it
> caused difficulties.[21]

One of the anomalies was that the 1920 Act made Northern
Ireland:

> a separate financial region, a self-financing region, by
> separating its revenues from national accounts, but at the same
> time denying it the power to raise whatever revenues were
> necessary for the proper government of the six counties. . . . It
> was . . . a strange system which originated not in Northern
> Ireland's needs but in the British Government's wishful
> thinking about the relationship it could establish with
> Southern Ireland.[22]

One of the few far-sighted Northern Ireland nationalists of the
1960s, John Duffy, spelled out the implications:

> the 1920 Act prevents Stormont from raising income, profits,
> capital or corporation profits taxes and also from levying
> customs and excise taxes. The 'transferred' taxes (i.e. those
> which Stormont has the power to levy) cover only such things
> as stamps and estate duties, motor taxes, entertainment taxes
> and a few other minor categories. The yield of the 'transferred'
> taxes is only about 15%. . . . Then again, Stormont has no
> power to control capital outflows . . . over £4,000,000,000 of
> Northern Ireland money is invested abroad – mostly in Britain.
> Stormont cannot vary the local bank rate, it is almost
> powerless to control the banking system and it is unable to
> protect new industries once they have been established here
> . . . the fiscal, monetary and physical disabilities outlined above
> seriously impair Stormont's capacity to tackle the chronic
> unemployment and underdevelopment problems which face
> us.

Duffy saw this as contributing to the internal divisions within
Northern Ireland. 'The two sections of the community are encouraged to retain the luxury of sectarianism as the basis of their political
allegiance.' For him, 'the present system actively militates against

any improvement in the quality of our political and social life'.[23]
Stormont had unfettered control over all the matters which enabled
the Unionists to discriminate and to perpetuate sectarianism, but no
control over the economic issues which might have cut across
communal divisions.

So Stormont was not truly independent; but it was not effectively
supervised either. Theoretically, Section 75 of the Government of
Ireland Act (1920) reserved supreme power over Northern Ireland to
the Westminster Parliament, but this meant nothing because no
government at Westminster wanted to take over responsibility for
Northern Ireland. In 1922 the Unionists faced down an attempt by
the superior government to stop them abolishing PR for local
government elections. When it became clear that Westminster could
have its way only by accepting the resignation of the Northern
Ireland Government, and imposing direct rule, Westminster backed
down. Its bluff had been called and it was not until the extremity of
near civil war in August 1969 that it reluctantly, and tardily, stepped
in.

The Government of Ireland Act came about because Westminster
wanted to disentangle the Irish question from British politics. Its
relationship to Northern Ireland was bad because it did not want to
have to take the kind of detailed interest in Northern Ireland affairs
which would have enabled it to use that power on behalf of the
oppressed Catholic minority. A similar relationship to a devolved
Scottish government could be just as damaging, except that the lack
of interest would lead it to ignore Scotland's need to be different.
Instead of benign neglect, we would probably have irritated inter-
ference.

Scotland should not be tempted down the blind alley of devolution
again. A parliament with independent revenue-raising powers and
with constitutionally entrenched autonomy is the minimum amount
of sovereignty which the Scottish people should seek to retrieve. But
the real debate on the matter has not yet begun. So far it has been
largely confined to Scotland, with only a tiny minority of English
well-wishers aware of how radically Scottish opinion has changed.
When the issue finally comes before Westminster the instinct of most
English politicians will be to expect what they will regard as a
reasonable compromise; this will almost certainly involve a
surrender on the issue of sovereignty. It is quite likely that the
weakness of Westminster's control over Northern Ireland will be
cited as a reason for retaining authority in London. It will be
important at this point not to be derailed by another version of the
West Lothian Question, and to be aware of exactly *why* devolution
failed in Northern Ireland.

Scotland and Ireland – or at least West Central Scotland and North East Ireland – share, in religious sectarianism, a major problem and a significant source of division. Sectarianism is a more powerful force than it appears on the surface; for generations it has been part of the culture of some of the most heavily industrialised and densely populated areas of Scotland. It is the problem that dare not speak its name; it is part of that culture to take it for granted, not to examine it, and to avoid discussing it. There is some logic in this attitude, but this reluctance to bring to the surface what everyone knows to be there is, itself, sectarian. When, moreover, attempts have been made to confront it, they have usually been based on crass oversimplifications.

One example was the playing of the 'green card' by the Shettleston branch of the SNP in the 1987 general election campaign. Catholics of Irish descent were targeted in a leafletting campaign designed to enlist their Irish nationalist sympathies on the side of Scottish nationalism. Regarded purely in electoral terms, it was not a success. In April, three months before the election, they claimed to be running at about 22.9% in their canvass returns, but they ended up with 12.7%, having pushed the SNP vote up by no more than 4.8%. This was not a statistically significant difference from the average increase for the SNP in Glasgow of 2.95% in this election. In the 1988 District Council elections, the SNP in the Shettleston constituency scored 23.61%, increasing their vote by 12.89% over the 1984 district result, *without* resorting to their earlier tactic.[24]

The episode caused some alarm. The leadership of the SNP was reported to be unhappy about the Shettleston branch's activities and there was a flurry of hostile comment in the Scottish press, which dubbed the Shettleston branch, 'the Provisional SNP'. This writer, responding from Belfast, wrote:

> Scotland can help to solve the Northern Ireland problem by showing us an example of a united community, working by democratic means to overcome the social and economic problems we have in common. If, for reasons of political expediency or sheer ignorance, sectarianism is put back on the agenda in Scotland, the possibility of a resolution of the conflict in Northern Ireland will be significantly diminished.[25]

Tom Gallagher suggested a positive alternative:

> . . . instead of playing up solidarity with Ireland . . . (they) would be better off arguing that Scotland is a multi-faceted community, that no group has a monopoly on Scottishness and that generations of Catholic Irish immigrants have contributed by their labour and strong sense of community to the soundness of the nation. Much better, therefore, to stress the

Catholics' sense of belonging than stoke up ancestral loyalties which would only add to the divisions which Scotland's enemies feed on.[26]

The Shettleston SNP had adopted their tactic partly in response to the Sam Campbell affair the previous summer. Campbell was a leading Labour councillor in Midlothian who shocked the Labour Party by speaking at an Orange rally, during which he gave vent to sectarian remarks and sang, 'Oh Give Me a Home Where There's No Pope of Rome'. It emerged that Campbell was a leading Orangeman and that he held deeply sectarian views, but in the context of the Labour Party and his work as a councillor, this had never been evident. This gives a clue to the nature of religious sectarianism: it is episodic, it is not a state of permanent hostility and perpetual conflict, it emerges in specific situations and can lie quiescent for long periods before erupting in confrontation or violence.

In understanding sectarianism it is necessary, first of all, to recognise its profound inarticulacy. As Seamus Heaney puts it:

'Religion's never mentioned here,' of course.
'You know them by their eyes,' and hold your tongue.
'One side's as bad as the other,' never worse.
Christ it's near time that some small leak was sprung

In the great dykes the Dutchman made
To dam the dangerous tide that followed Seamus.
Yet for all this art and sedentary trade
I am incapable. The famous

Northern reticence, the tight gag of place
And times: yes, yes. Of the 'wee six' I sing
Where to be saved you only must save face
And whatever you say, you say nothing.[27]

Rosemary Harris, in her pioneering study of an Ulster rural community, cites an example of this inability to speak about what is evident:

coming one day into Mary Jamison's kitchen I found there a woman and a young boy who were strangers to me helping Mary with odd jobs. The woman was not introduced to me nor to Mary's in-laws when they came into the room – no one except Mary seemed able even to see the woman, and the only conversation consisted of stilted remarks made by the in-laws to each other or Mary. The woman spoke only to Mary and only in whispers, and the whole atmosphere was extraordinarily frigid.

It turned out that the woman and her son were Catholics. She was the widow of a Protestant who, although never officially changing

his religion, had been buried in a Catholic cemetery and in another
district. A former school-friend of Mary's, she was now in serious
financial difficulties and was being given temporary casual work as
an act of kindness.

> Mary's in-laws . . . who had never known the woman as a
> neighbour . . . were outraged and affronted by her presence.
> They displayed no hostility towards the boy, but refused to
> speak to his mother, and she continued to exhibit timid, almost
> fearful, self-effacement.[28]

What should be noted about this episode is the highly symbolic
nature of the woman's offence. She had behaved as if her husband
was 'one of her own', and had denied him the proper rituals and the
burial place of his community. It should also be noted that the
hostility was extremely economical. No one wanted to extend it to
the boy, and Mary's charity was not directly criticised. The woman
herself accepted the situation and behaved in as unobtrusive a way as
possible. Everyone dealt with the problem as an unfortunate
disruption of the normal course of life, best dealt with by ignoring it
as much as possible until it was over.

It is in the nature of the thing that sectarianism should be highly
correlated with another long-standing social problem – drink. Often
it is only alcohol which can loosen the tongue and break down
inhibitions sufficiently for the deep strata of antagonism to break
through to the surface. An incident from Northern Ireland in the
1960s illustrates the point. In January 1966 a publican in Tandragee,
Co. Armagh, was convicted of an arson attack on a local Catholic
church. He had been drinking until the early hours of the morning
and suddenly 'took a notion'. He ran over to the church, threw a mug
of paraffin over the door and set it alight. Then he broke a window
and pushed a paraffin-soaked lighted shirt through it. He had also
draped a Union flag over the church railings, and a passing milkman,
who saw this, commented, 'That's a bad business'. The publican
replied, 'It will give them something to talk about.'[29]

This exchange is loaded with unexpressed meaning. The milkman
is deeply disturbed by what he sees as a dangerous provocation and
wants to make his disapproval clear. The publican by now feels
guilty, and thinks it necessary to offer, not a justification, but a semi-
jocular comment. But neither can discuss what has happened, it is in
the category of facts which are not in the public domain. Both know
that there has been a breach of sectarian etiquette, but the same
etiquette demands that they do not talk about it. And they learned
these rules, not by being told about them, but by hints and signs
which they absorbed in childhood and which they do not even know
as rules; they are simply what is *done*.

The sectarian culture of Northern Ireland does not imply popular endorsement of bitterness and hostility between the two communities, quite the reverse. The 1969 Loyalty Survey carried out by Strathclyde University found that 82% of respondents thought that people in Northern Ireland should try to forget the past and look to the future. 65% of Protestants and 66% of Catholics thought that it was important not to give offence in dealing with the other community.[30] The events of August 1969, however, show that such ideas are similar to attitudes to original sin; it is a condition from which they would like to escape, but they know that this aspiration cannot be achieved in this world, nor by any actions of their own.

Many of the most striking aspects of sectarianism in Northern Ireland – residential segregation, divining the other person's religion from discrete signs, involvement in different sports and social activities, informal restriction of different occupations to Protestants or Catholics – are control mechanisms, which limit the contact between members of the two communities. When they do come into contact there are elaborate, but unwritten rules of conduct about not giving offence. This is why Northern Ireland people are constantly protesting to outsiders about how well they get on with each other. Sectarianism is a means, precisely, of ensuring that this will be the case. But it is a dangerously flawed mechanism for maintaining peace. It perpetuates ignorance and prejudice within each community about the other, it perpetuates inequality, with Catholics relegated to a less favoured position, and it breaks down from time to time because existing custom and practice are not strong enough to maintain the balance between the two communities when some new and unexpected challenge to the status quo appears. In this way it perpetuates violence and the potential for violence.

There are important differences between sectarianism in Ireland and Scotland. In Scotland territoriality is insignificant, sectarianism has very little impact on politics and is most evidently manifested in the context of football. The writer's subjective impression is that Scottish sectarianism is more open and blatant and more inclined to flaunt itself in front of the other community. But in both countries it is a profoundly complex phenomenon which requires painstaking study and thought if it is to be understood and combated. But, whereas in Northern Ireland a great deal of highly informative work has been done, such an effort has scarcely started in Scotland. Scots should learn from Northern Ireland and begin to study the problem *before* it explodes in the faces of those who want to maintain the unity of all Scotland's people.

Modern Scotland has not shared in the Irish tradition of political violence. This is something to be profoundly thankful for, but it should not be taken for granted. Like the absence of serious sectarian trouble, this is largely because the conditions for its appearance have not emerged. It is innocence, not calculation, which has maintained a non-violent tradition. As Owen Dudley Edwards puts it:

> The question of violence is central to what happened in Ireland, both to the official aridity which settled on the country and the endless spate of murder which now is the curse of Northern Ireland. It had other effects. In my youth it was very difficult to encounter a self-styled nationalist of my generation who was not an opportunist or a moron. It was, therefore, with a wonderful sense of rebirth that I discovered an implacably non-violent nationalism when I came to Scotland. It seemed like discovering the Garden of Eden before the Fall.[31]

Scotland *could* fall. The smugness, arrogance and self-satisfaction of the present government at Westminster, and its closing off of every avenue for constitutional redress of Scotland's grievances, closely parallel the situation which gave rise to the civil rights movement in Northern Ireland. There too, the Unionist government refused to concede that there was any legitimate cause for complaint and the political system blocked off every channel but street protests. The civil rights movement was deeply committed to non-violence, but its leadership lacked the experience and knowledge with which to sustain a non-violent strategy so that the deep-rooted violence within the Irish political culture finally overcome it.[32] The Scots do not have this violent tradition, but there are dangers. The violence in Northern Ireland was not caused by Irish traditions, they merely shaped it when it appeared. The violence itself arose from uncontrolled anger, hasty responses to provocation and the lack of a coherent alternative.

If, as the *Claim of Right* document seeks to show, the present constitutional framework does not allow Scotland to obtain redress of its grievances, a struggle for justice will, by definition, have to be unconstitutional, and will have to involve passive resistance and civil disobedience. Such a struggle contains within it a potential for violence. A non-violent strategy does not imply the absence of strong antagonisms; on the contrary it seeks to use the tension created by the potential for violence to obtain change by other means. But if violence actually occurs it dissipates that tension and defeats the whole purpose of the strategy. Moreover a victory won by violence would not be worth having. It would only be a temporary statement of the balance of forces at a particular time. The bitterness engendered by the violence would ensure that, sooner or later, the matter would be contested again. Scotland must not be allowed to slip into the downward spiral of mutually reinforcing outrage which has characterised relations between Britain and Ireland and within Ireland itself. If violence occurs the proponents of Scottish self-government must ensure that it is inflicted *on* them and not *by* them. In the words of Terence MacSwiney, the murdered Lord Mayor of Cork, 'It is not those who can inflict the most, but those that can suffer the most who will conquer.'

There are positive lessons to be learned from Ireland. The courage and self-sacrifice of many Irish nationalists. The intellectual brilliance of political writers and activists like Fintan Lalor, Michael Davitt and James Connolly. The integrity of those who constructed a modern democracy out of the civil war-torn society of Southern Ireland. The heroism in face of immense adversity of those who created the Irish Labour Movement. The determination of women like Constance Markievicz, Louis Bennet, Helena Moloney and Winnie Carney who ensured that women could have a place in the forefront of Irish politics, despite a profoundly misogynist time and culture. The enhanced dignity and independence which the Republic of Ireland has acquired since it decided to share its sovereignty in the European Community. The endurance of those in Northern Ireland who have not allowed hope to be smothered by violence.

Despite all the mistakes and false turnings, the struggle for an independent Ireland was justified, and has created a better nation than there would have been, had the Irish bowed to superior force. Scotland should learn from that example too.

6

The SNP and the Lure of Europe

ISOBEL LINDSAY

For a nationalist party, developments in the European Community involve an inherent dilemma. The drive for national self-determination and the push towards greater centralised supranationalism present obvious tensions. They may be partially reconcilable but they are tensions of a dynamic nature which are likely to reproduce in a wider context many of the problems which have resulted in Scottish dissatisfaction with the Union. One of the inevitable disadvantages of the party system is the reluctance to give them open recognition to meet dilemmas. Manifestos are expected to display clear-cut solutions and enthusiasms not to put creative tension on offer as an option. This has produced serious deficiencies in the political debate on Scotland and the European dimension. For short-term expediency, the 'Scotland in Europe' concept was projected as an easy escape route from the problems of seeking a constitutional settlement with England, an escape into a utopia in which strong influence could be wielded and generous regional grants received, where great change could be achieved without much being changed. The 'Scotland in Europe' debate which needs to take place has to be based on a realistic assessment of the great problems Scotland faces as a small peripheral nation operating in the context of powerful trends towards economic concentration and centralisation, both in the public and the private spheres, in Western Europe. It needs also to look in breadth at the nature of Scotland's internationalism and at what special contribution, if any, Scotland can make. The radical changes taking place in Eastern Europe and the Soviet Union have dramatically highlighted the narrowness of the focus in much of the European debate of the past twenty years. It gives us the opportunity to think ahead in a broader perspective. What should Scotland as a small northern European nation, part of Europe's 'top storey', be seeking in her international role?

The international dimension has been of enormous importance to

Scots. In many respects it has and continues to be more important to Scots than to Scotland as an entity. The high propensity of Scots to work outwith Scotland has been one of the most consistent features of our history. In the early modern period, continental Europe was the principal location for that migration. From the fifteenth to the seventeenth century there was extensive movement to Poland, Prussia, Sweden, France, Finland, the Netherlands and Ireland. Then the direction changed. The Unions of 1603 and 1707 opened up movement to England, then North America, Australia, India, Africa, the Far and Middle East, significantly changing the orientation of Scots. Much of that change is still with us; the personal international ties are woven into Scottish society and are regularly reinforced. If we looked at the personal 'maps' of five million Scots, we would see an impressive pattern of international linkages, still heavily weighted towards the traditional receiving countries. This is the accumulated result of the last two hundred years. It may have arisen from the failures of Scottish society but it constitutes a strong biographical internationalism which we should try to develop as an asset by encouraging cultural, political and economic links developed out of personal ties. In this respect Scotland is not unique but it is special. We are a nation facing in many directions and we should not under-play that specialness by concentrating exclusively on the European context.

The European Community brings into focus the various ideological positions underpinning contemporary nationalism. Because of the sensitivity of the issues of nationalism versus supra-nationalism and the question-mark it places over the nature of sovereignty, the issue challenges nationalist rationale. What are these different ideological positions and how have they responded? We can readily identify four, not neatly self-contained in practice but distinct enough to be recognisable. The first is a romantic, sometimes semi-mystical, concept of nationhood, legitimised by length of history and communal experience. Strong on the rhetoric of freedom and cultural distinctiveness. The second is a small state nationalism as part of the process of decentralising power structures, creating a new kind of democratic ethos with related economic values, perhaps now more easily identifiable as nationalism with shades of green. The third is nationalism as 'Left' politics, as a route to a state more socialist in its values. People in this category might not be nationalist in Bavaria but are happy to be so in Scotland. The fourth is nationalism as modernisation, as a response to uneven development. A perception of Scotland as economically and socially backward. A desire to join some 'premier league' but with no clear Left-Right dimension.

These are, of course, 'ideal type' constructs. Individuals might overlap in their orientation but these have been distinguishable strands in nationalist politics since the sixties. The EC presents very real problems for the first and second of these positions and some for the third but it fits readily with the fourth. If as in the first category, independence is felt to be an unquestionable right and nationalism to be the correct basis from which to develop political systems, it is difficult to accept solutions which are inherently federalist in their direction. Models of federal structures for the UK have been rejected by them as failing to give both adequate powers to Scotland and also true freedom in some spiritual sense. Therefore the post-1992 EC with its drive to greater integration and supranationalism conflicts with the basis of their political philosophy.

The second position produces a different dilemma. If small-state nationalism is about bringing control closer to people, if it is part of a new democratic agenda, can it legitimately welcome an EC which represents a growing bureaucratic centralism and which economically seeks to create the condition which will facilitate larger-scale industrial, commercial and financial institutions? The rationale of the Single European Act is to do just that, to produce economic and social conditions which will create supposed economic benefits of a scale by offering a large standardised labour market, readily mobile, and a product market unfettered by any national protectionism or differential standards. The assumption is that this will create a smaller number of larger economic organisations which can be more internationally competitive. The basic logic of this approach is part of the standard economic defence of British unionism, i.e. that large economic organisations developed out of large markets are essential for economic well-being, and that, therefore, the appropriate level of political control should be at the appropriate market level. The opposition of many modern Greens both on the continent and in the UK to the EC is based on an analysis which suggests that the large multi-national manufacturing and commercial corporations require constantly expanding consumerism for their profitability and survival. Also that the attempt to impose standardised economic conditions on very diverse situations, whether the Common Agricultural Policy or Stalinist-type command economic planning, is likely to produce a wasteful (and often corrupt) use of resources. The new democratic agenda requires power and initiative to come closer to people and policies to be varied and flexible to meet different environments and priorities. This does not fit comfortably with the direction in which the EC is moving and produces contradictions both ideological and pragmatic which are difficult to resolve.

For those principally motivated by nationalism as Left politics, the approach to the EC may be more ambivalent. There are those on the Left who have seen the possibility of building and using a Left alliance in the EC to push through social and economic changes in an egalitarian direction. There are other sections on the Left who regard the free market basis, the power to prevent intervention at national level, the supranational restrictions on monetary and fiscal policy, the free movement of capital, etc. as greatly restricting the economic options open to any government of the Left. In the Scottish context behind both interpretations is the assumption that there will be a UK government of the Right, or at least to the right of any government that Scotland on its own would produce, thus justifying the independence route.

The fourth position – nationalism as modernisation – is the one which fits most comfortably into a pro-EC stance. Modernisation involves an implicit comparative conception of what is 'best', best in terms of levels of consumption, best in terms of education, health, transport, etc. This 'bestness' is ideologically eclectic; bestness in different types of social systems may be used for comparative purposes. All contrasts are used to reinforce the notion of disadvantaged development. If the central concern is retarded or disadvantaged development, then the prospect of the independent membership of an increasingly powerful EC is seen as being part of this process of modernisation, of being associated with the important and powerful, of having seats at top tables. Nationalism as modernisation is not particularly concerned with cultural distinctiveness. On the contrary since much of which is best is seen as happening elsewhere and is what we should aspire to, the distinctiveness aspect is of little importance. Nor is it particularly concerned with the nature of power structures. It is simply measurable results which matter. It does not have a committed ideological position on the Left-Right spectrum, just a rather magpie-like pragmatism. This type of orientation to nationalism finds the prospect of standardisation in many respects attractive since it provides the antidote to feelings of relative deprivation. In the conventional wisdom, supranational developments are seen as progressive and multinational industrial and financial institutions are accepted as an inevitable part of the modernisation process. This is the strand of nationalism which found it easy to be positively enthusiastic about post-1992 developments in the EC and which was the most dominant in the SNP by the end of the eighties.

One important aspect of the SNP's 'Scotland in Europe' position has been the theme of the EC as escape. This has had three aspects: using the EC as a means of gaining independence by bypassing Westminster, escaping finally from the separatist attack, and finding

a way out of practical and psychological dependence on England.
The independence through Europe argument was a major part of the
SNP's recent campaigning, especially in the 1989 Euro Elections.
The scenario presented was that voting for the SNP would establish
a mandate for independence if it gained a majority. This would be
recognised as legitimate by other EC members and from this position
independent-member status could be negotiated which would
overrule objections from the British state. The latter would be forced
to concede independence as a result of this pressure. The route to
independence would, therefore, not be dependent on Westminster
decisions and England could be bypassed.

Rather surprisingly much of the discussion on independence in
Europe, in particular the attacks on it, were centred around the
question of whether a Scottish state would be accepted as an independent member. Could England veto it? Would membership be
automatic or would Scotland have to apply as any other new
member would? Principally Conservative, but some Labour
politicians also, leaned heavily on the argument that independent
Scottish membership would not be automatic, that Scotland might
be excluded, that it would create a period of uncertainty. Nationalist
politicians on the other hand argued that there would be no reason
to exclude Scotland, that influential legal advice supported this, that
if Scotland had to apply, so would England since both would have a
changed identity. The interesting point about this argument was the
failure of Conservative and Labour politicians to focus on the
genuinely weak point in it rather than pursuing what came to be an
increasingly esoteric and legalistic dispute.[1] The argument that other
EC states, including England, would reject the membership of a
Scottish state which had negotiated a settlement with the British
government, was always implausible. If a British government had
accepted the transfer of sovereignty to Scotland with a separate
constitution and a duly elected Scottish parliament, there would be
no significant political or economic reason for such a rejection. But
the situation is entirely different if it is envisaged that other EC states
would somehow overrule the UK and recognise Scotland as an
independent member state on the basis of election results without a
negotiated settlement with Westminster. This is totally implausible
because it would establish a precedent with profound implications.
It would in effect mean that the EC could alter the boundaries of
member states in response to the expressed wishes of sections of the
electorate in any state. Spain, Belgium, France, could all be vulnerable to such demands if a precedent were established. The response
of a British government, especially one hostile even to a modest,
devolved legislature, would be to argue that this was an internal

issue for the UK as a whole and that there was no constitutional right of secession.

The election of a majority of MPs and MEPs favouring independence may constitute a moral mandate but it does not constitute a power base. Without a negotiated settlement involving the agreement of Westminster, even if a reluctant consent, there is no control over financial and economic resources, no control over a civil service. It is certainly possible to envisage a period in which various forms of civilian resistance involving extensive trade union, local authority and other institutional and popular support for that moral mandate, might compel a Westminster government to make major concessions but this would be a process which would require a very broad-based and united coalition of interests in Scotland and the outcome might be something less than immediate independence. Certainly the external pressure of other countries might create sufficient embarrassment to add to the pressure for change. But the EC does not offer any quick escape route which avoids the process of reaching a prior settlement with England.

Whatever the hostility the present UK government might have created among other member-states, it is one of the major players. It would be counter-productive for other states to 'play the Scottish card' and totally antagonise a large state with important markets for the sake of a potential minor one. It would involve the EC in interfering in a way not covered by existing community law and in giving support to a shadow government which did not have full legal or de facto control over what was happening in its own territory. In the scenario of actually getting to independence as distinct from persuading people of its desirability, the EC dimension offers nothing new. To achieve a domestic legislature with an established institutional structure still seems a much stronger base from which to negotiate independence than seeking to go straight to independence from the base of thirty-seven MPs.

The EC was also seen as a way of escaping from the charge of separatism, a bogey word from the late sixties and seventies which had become the parrot-like response of opponents to the challenge of Scottish nationalism, a response requiring no analysis only image. The image was one of isolation, of being cut off from others, of being without support. The implied threat was that there would be restrictions on commercial and industrial trading. The anxiety response to the word did not, of course, stand up to intellectual scrutiny. The existence of extensive international trading agreements provided a rational rebuttal to the threat of punitive sanctions following independence. But separatism was not primarily about rational concerns but about irrational anxiety. The fear of responsibility, of having no one to fall back on, of facing the unknown were at the heart of the response to the separatist attack. Independence in Europe was seen as a way of countering this anxiety both at a rational and an emotional level. Rationally because it provided a formal guarantee against commercial discrimination in relation to other EC countries, especially England. Emotionally because it projected the image of being part of a larger entity and not solely responsible for ourselves, achieving independence while minimising change, rejecting dependency while clinging to dependency. Ambivalence is a readily understandable human response to the challenge of change. But for those seeking change with the reassurance of continuity, independence in the EC may still be less attractive than a domestic legislature within the familiar UK umbrella. Especially since the EC is not a particularly popular institution with which people identify. In a poll carried out just before the 1989 Euro Elections, a clear majority of Scottish respondents thought that the EC had reduced Scotland's control over her destiny, failed to make Scotland more prosperous than she would otherwise have been and had made food prices go up. Only 11% thought that the SNP had the best policies on Europe, well below their share of the party votes.[2] For the anxious, a domestic legislature offers substantial change but greater reassurance, while for those psychologically or politically attracted to radical change, the addition of the EC factor at this stage may make little difference. Indeed this is clearly supported by polling evidence.[3] Where a poll has offered a full range of constitutional options, as the Scottish Mori polls have done, support for independence both inside and outside the EC has been around one-third, little different from what it was earlier in the eighties before the Independence in Europe campaign. Only if the question is asked as a choice between independence in the EC and the status quo, without giving a range of opinions, do you get significantly higher support.[4] So at this stage the EC as an escape from separatism may be insufficiently risk-free for some sections of the electorate and may add little to the appeal of independence for the enthusiasts for change. It might, of course, become a more important factor in influencing opinion were independence on offer tomorrow.

The European context was also seen as escape from the cultural and political dominance of the south, an attempt to change the central reference group for Scots away from London and towards other European societies. There is, of course, nothing especially new in this. It has been a recurring preoccupation of nationalist groups to try to stimulate interest in developments in other small countries in order to heighten aspirations and increase confidence. It was a long-standing cliché of nationalist rhetoric to compare Scotland with the

Scandinavian countries and to contrast the international connections and achievements of Scots at a personal level to the narrow
horizons of the Scottish political community. SNP policy documents
from the seventies were strongly internationalist in orientation and
visitors from e.g. Catalonia, Quebec, Denmark, spoke at functions.
How much of this reached the broader public is a different matter.
The Scottish electorate seemed more receptive to a political message
which was reinforced by comparisons of how Scotland fared vis-a-
vis the more prosperous parts of England or which highlighted the
insensitivity of the south to Scottish affairs. There was, therefore,
always the problem that Scottish nationalism would define itself in
opposition to English nationalism because no matter the concern to
encourage a broader international perspective, political expediency
and media interests would channel attention towards the Scottish-
English relationship.

The growing power of the EC over national governments and its
generally higher profile was seen as an opportunity to stress the
declining significance of Westminster and a need for the reorientation of Scotland towards the continent. England would not
have to be psychologically confronted as a dominant influence so
much as psychologically bypassed. We could write off the
significance of the south as a backwater rather than challenge it. One
difficulty with this approach is that whatever its strengths in theory,
it may seem very abstract to the public. The current issues of live
concern – the poll-tax, employment, the health service, education,
social security – are perceived correctly as issues which have to be
fought out with Westminster. They are evidence of the continued
strength of the South. The eighties have probably produced a
stronger sense of subordination to London-based government than
ever before. It is this heightened awareness of its power to impose
deeply unpopular policies on a sullenly hostile Scotland which has
strengthened the support for Scottish nationalism. There is no
popular feeling of the declining power of UK government; rather one
of stubborn, naked and insensitive power. This reduces the street-
wise credibility of the notion that there is an easy way to alter the
preoccupation with the Scottish-English relationship. You cannot
both build it up as a threat, as the source of Scotland's disadvantaged
position, and then expect it to be psychologically plausible to argue
that attention should be shifted from the Westminster relationship
because of the greater importance of the European.

Thus the EC as an escape route, a constitutional escape route, an
escape from separatism, and a psychological escape from UK-
orientation, has more superficial plausibility than it has substance.

Contemporary Scottish nationalism has been dominated by the

relative advantages and disadvantages for the Scottish economy of constitutional change. Although the unpopularity of a range of Conservative legislation in the eighties has pushed the focus from time to time onto education, health, housing, all of these debates have also had an economic aspect. Therefore the implications of the EC for the economic case for independence is a central one. A useful starting point is to go back to the basic economic case for dissatisfaction with the Union. The nationalist argument has always been that Scotland suffered economically from the Union especially in the twentieth century because the economic interests of the centre were frequently not the same as the economic interests of the periphery. The dominant economy of the SE might be overheated and require deflationary monetary and fiscal policy, while the Scottish economy was still emerging from recession. It was the interests of the central economy which regularly prevailed. Therefore without independence in monetary and fiscal policy allowing for an economic sensitivity to the particular needs of Scotland, it becomes difficult to achieve an optimum performance. A second problem was thought to be the centralised control of production and distribution, whether in the public or private sectors and the problems this creates for non-favoured areas. From the perspective of the centre a smaller number of larger production units, e.g. in steel, may be preferable but from the perspective of areas which lose production the disadvantages predominate. Centralised purchasing may have considerable benefits from one vantage point but may damage the viability of smaller-scale localised production. Thirdly the centralisation of political power, it has been argued, brings with it the geographical centralisation of much economic activity and the physical concentration of an unduly high proportion of the most skilled and best paid employment.

These have been the central arguments for the nationalist economic critique of the Union. The debate about the direction of the flow of subsidy in public revenue and expenditure, despite its higher profile, has been subsidiary to the more sophisticated arguments about the need for flexible, independent, economic tools which could be applied to strengthen a peripheral economy in opposition to the interests and powers of the centre. The counter-arguments of those supporting the economic results of the Union were that easy access to wider markets, membership of a larger trading bloc combined with regional policies were to Scotland's advantage and provided the economic justification for staying in the UK. Apart from those with an uncritical faith in the free market, it was argued that the problems of the centralising trends within the UK could adequately be counter-balanced by a range of regional economic strategies to encourage industrial development, improve infra-structure, etc. as a compensation for the admitted disadvantages for peripheral economies of standardised central monetary and fiscal policies and large-scale production units. The nationalist argument against regional policies as an adequate substitute for wider economic powers, was that they were generally marginal in contrast to the problems created by central economic management and that they created a dependency mentality which strengthened the political hold of the centre since the centre had the power of economic patronage. There was always a degree of ambivalence towards regional policies since on the one hand it was recognised as desirable to get what was possible out of the system and channel resources into Scotland, but on the other it legitimised a 'sleight of hand' which deprived Scotland of resources through inappropriate economic policies and returned some resources as 'gifts' generously given and for which the more deprived areas had to compete with each other.

This debate was waged in the late sixties and seventies between those supporting centralised economic powers modified by regional policies as the most effective strategy and those supporting the need for the control of economic powers by a Scottish state. It was a perfectly legitimate debate on both sides and one in which there were no simple winners and losers in the argument. In the late eighties this debate took an unusual twist when the SNP chose to embrace not reluctantly but with enthusiasm the necessity and inevitability of a very substantial centralisation of economic powers on a Western European basis offset by regional policies. Just as in the seventies there were legitimate arguments on different sides, so there is in the context of the nineties. They are essentially the same arguments. On the integrationist side the arguments are for the need for the standardised mass domestic market in order to encourage maximum economies of scale and compete more effectively with the Japanese and the US. To create a standardised product market, you require a standardised labour market with similarities in working conditions and unrestricted movement of labour. You require the harmonisation of indirect taxation, of aid to industry, of company taxation and commercial law, of competition and mergers policy, of monetary policy, of public procurement policy. As Bryan Gould has commented:

> The real damage will come, however, from the fact that the closer we move to a single European economy, the more like a single economy it will behave. In other words productive capacity within that single economy will tend to concentrate in the most productive parts, leaving the rest as a depressed

periphery, such as we are familiar with in smaller national economies. . . . However much the EC spends on social and regional policy, it will pale into significance by comparison with the huge power of the market forces we have unleashed.[5]

As in the British strategy of the sixties and seventies, it is recognised that to encourage economies of scale and to facilitate concentration, there will be considerable damage to some areas which need to be offset by centrally financed regional projects.

The opposing critique of this scenario questions the assumption that the very large standardised domestic market is a prerequisite for commercial success. Japan has a domestic market about half that of the United States and about a third of the EC. A number of countries with small domestic markets have produced high living standards and reasonably stable economies. Only if we moved into a highly protectionist period would the smaller domestic market constitute an insurmountable problem. Indeed because a small state requires a very small share of international markets to prosper, the elasticity of demand for its products is potentially greater and the important factor is its ability to use strategies to produce and promote attractive products. As J. K. Galbraith pointed out twenty years ago, the drive for economic concentration in the private sector has more to do with reducing competition and risk than it has with technical economies of scale.[6] It may be more advantageous for the small national or region to exercise maximum discretion and flexibility in economic policy, to use its advantage of being able to 'jump like frogs' as suggested in the recent report of the Standing Commission on the Scottish Economy.[7]

The justification of the Single Market as something required to give a stimulus to economic concentration in order to improve competitiveness, suggests that we are operating with a political agenda dictated by the interests of multi-national capital. Whether it turns out to be in the interests of the people, or of some sections of the people, is incidental.

The notion that greater concentration of supranational power in the EC is justified because of the need to control multi-national companies, a popular argument on the Left, requires critical scrutiny. The past twenty years, a period of growing power and influence for the EC, has also been a period of unprecedented concentration of private economic power. This has not been contained; it has thrived. It is universally accepted that 1992 will give a boost to this process. So the power of the multi-national will be encouraged. How does this help the process of control? The large corporate firms have proved very difficult to restrict because they control so much employment and given the very high and competitive demand for that employment, they have the trump card.

It is the diversification of economic power in the private sector rather than its concentration which is likely to give greater potential for control on behalf of the public interest. To pursue policies whose justification is to create market conditions which encourage a smaller number of larger companies in order to produce supposed economies of scale, seems to be counter-productive in seeking to restrict that massive private power.

It would be argued from the current mainstream nationalist position, that membership of the EC as an independent state is a fundamentally different relationship in economic and other respects from that within the UK. That is certainly the case in relation to a range of non-economic functions but the post-1992 relationship, if the script goes as planned, would leave little more influence or discretion in key economic areas. With three out of seventy-nine of the weighted votes in the Council of Ministers, 3% of the seats in the European Parliament, 1.5% of the population, Scotland's position would clearly be a minor one. Even in the areas in which the veto technically continues, it has now become obviously a mythical power. For a small state the most that can be expected in the nineties is an influence probably little different in kind from that exercised by the Scottish Secretary in the British Cabinet, not negligible but rarely central. There is, therefore, in the economic spheres a legitimate comparison between the relationships of Scotland in the UK and Scotland in the EC as it is developing.

The strength of the 'Independence in Europe' slogan lies in the need for a nationalist movement to have an internationalist vision. An important part of the case for seeking independence rather than a domestic parliament is the opportunity it offers to act in an international capacity and develop a distinctive international role. To offer an inspirational projection of that role is both legitimate and challenging. But while visions may be allowed some poetic licence, they must also stand up to scrutiny. Independent membership of an increasingly integrationist EC is more striking for its continuity than as a radical departure. Once the merit of independence as opposed to a domestic legislature is seen as primarily a better way of exerting influence on the EC, then the argument becomes a balance-sheet, not a principle, not part of a broader democratic ideology. With a Westminster government which owes Scotland no political debts and which is hostile to mainstream Scottish aspirations, that balance-sheet of influence comes down on the independence side. But if the Westerminster government was one which did owe Scotland a political debt and was consequently more attentive to Scottish interests, the balance sheet could look different. On the one hand you would have independent membership as a small state with much modest bargaining power; on the other you would have representation via a large state with much greater bargaining potential which you might expect to be used some of the time in Scotland's interests. Under those circumstances the balance sheet might still favour independent membership but it would certainly not be clear-cut. If this capacity to exert influence in the EC is made the flagship of your independence case against that of a domestic legislature, it could prove to be very vulnerable to changing political circumstances.

In looking for a fresh vision of Scotland's internationalism the starting point should be an assessment of what Scotland has to contribute in an international context. There are three particular factors which are a starting point. One is a sensitivity based on historical experience of the negative effects of the externalisation of control and initiative. The second is an ecological-strategic position as part of the European 'top storey'. The third is a very broadly based internationalism which has come from those accumulated personal biographies and which transcends a narrow Western European perspective. Whatever situation Scotland finds itself in, whatever institutional choices it makes, these distinctive aspects of Scottish internationalism should be kept to the fore.

It is somewhat ironic that at a time when the lessons from the Soviet Union and Eastern Europe are of the stultifying effects of concentrating power at the centre, creating massive institutions with little public accountability, pushing mass standardisation rather than diversity, the trends we are asked to believe are inevitable in Western Europe are exactly these. The suggestion that the EC might develop into a loose confederal structure, a Europe of the Regions, a Europe of the Fifty, has proved very difficult to translate into institutional structures even at a theoretical level without producing a fully-fledged federal system on the one hand or simply a system of permanent regional lobbying institutions on the other. Certainly current EC trends make this more difficult. The German Lander have expressed concern at the increasing encroachment of EC powers into areas which are their constitutional responsibility. Even those whose basic political philosophy is concerned with democratisation and who want to interpret current trends optimistically, produce rather questionable scenarios. Neal Ascherson, for example, concedes that:

> The outer skin of the European Community is going to become thicker and harder . . . the integrated Community will acquire the right to make almost all foreign policy decisions, economic and political, on behalf of its members . . . accordingly national domestic policies within the EC – even those which are not due to be harmonised and run centrally from Brussels – will grow defenceless and eventually impracticable.[8]

Even if these trends are somewhat counter-balanced by the extension of various forms of regionalism, it is an uneven balance in terms of the gulf between the individual, the local community and the centre. While positively supporting European co-operation in certain spheres, Scotland's experience ought to put it firmly in an anti-integrationist position, the Europe of Nations, not the Mitterand vision of the Franco-German-led Western European super-state. The principle of keeping as much initiative as we can as close to people as we can, of valuing democratic responsibility over patronage, even if that patronage is often benign, seems a good basis for a Scottish approach to internationalism, and one which may find an echoing response in Eastern Europe.

An enthusiastic Scotland in Europe campaign cannot cover up these difficult and contentious debates in which sides have to be taken. The problem is that once the European relationship is perceived as a difficult and contentious one, it loses its simple appeal, it becomes problem politics not escape politics. Thus it has become a regular response from the SNP to the problems arising out of EC policies on agriculture, fishing, land ownership, industrial support etc., to brush them aside as problems which will be solved by bargaining power, use of the veto, derogation, declaration of vital national interests. There are, however, no simple or guaranteed solutions to externally imposed policies we don't like. The discretion would not rest with us; we could only hope there would be better representation of our interests based on influence, not power. There have been some recent signs of unease in nationalist ranks. Foreign affairs spokesperson Alan Macartney has recently stated:

> One suspects that the Delors vision is of a United States of Europe which would be a transatlantic version of the USA, whose existence and federal constitution exert a mesmeric force on Euro-fanatics. . . . Our preference is for a loose confederation.[9]

This would put the SNP on a collision course with the current direction of change. It is a perfectly reasonable position to argue that Scotland should seek independent membership of the EC but should be committed to fight against the currently dominant trends but this was hardly the tenor of the Scotland in Europe campaign.

Recent events in the Soviet Union and Eastern Europe have given a more realistic perspective to what had become an increasingly inturned Western Europe debate. We need to take a bolder, less conservative look at Europe as a whole and at Scotland's place in it. The currently most pressing need at the European level is for the development of Pan-European institutional structures which will provide a forum for conflict resolution, security issues and ecological co-operation. We urgently need a model for the whole of Europe which is much closer to a European United Nations rather than a European United States. The basis for such a development lies in adapting and envigorating the Helsinki process in order to fill the vacuum positively which will develop with the dissolution of the military blocs. The concept of an increasingly tightly-integrated Western European state facing a still substantially integrated Soviet Union with sections of Eastern Europe floating somewhere in the middle, is a great missed opportunity, not least in the light of Scotland's interests.

Scotland's natural geophysical position, her ecological setting is as part of the 'top storey' of the common European home. Ths 'top storey' encompasses Finland, Sweden, Norway, Iceland, Denmark, the North West Soviet Union, including the Baltic states. These were, of course, countries with which early modern Scotland had strong links of trade and migration. Today there are many shared interests and problems. There are common strategic problems in an area whose waters have the world's highest concentration of nuclear submarines. There are common ecological problems affecting particularly forestry and fishing. With the likelihood of an increasing degree of independence for the Soviet Baltic states, this is an area in which the small state has a central role to play, not a peripheral one and where culturally and politically there is much in common. The Soviet Union has particular import needs in advanced engineering and electronics and in food products. All of this suggests a potentially fruitful and distinctive international role for Scotland in the European context. The concept of a 'top-storey' axis in northern Europe and possibly a Mediterranean axis, could produce a much more balanced pattern of European relationships than having massive power focused on a German-dominated west central Europe. The notion of a Europe of many circles under the umbrella of a Pan-European forum coincides both with the interests of Scotland and the needs of Europe in the nineties. It provides appropriate structures for security and co-operation, discourages super-state aspirations and allows voluntaristic and varied patterns of inter-state relationships to develop.

The third contribution which Scotland can make on the international front is to build on that genuine biographical internationalism. The great risk we face today is that an in-turned Soviet Union, an in-turned United States and an in-turned Europe are going to be much less concerned with cultivating the poor majority in the world. The North-South communication gap could increase as the East-West gap narrows. If these developments limit neo-colonial intervention, they might have a plus side. But there is little likelihood of the economic exploitation diminishing. Scotland's role could never be more than modest but it could be positive, especially in educational aid. The North American and Australasian connection offer opportunities for increased economic and cultural links which a Scottish government would be well placed to developed.

If we argue that Scotland has a positive role to play internationally as an anti-centralist, small northern European nation with strong global links, what are the institutional implications? Are we in a period in which nationalism as statism is in rapid decline and instead do we face a period of institutional post-nationalism, a post-nationalism in which not just Scotland as a region but regions in Scotland might regard themselves as the more important players *vis-à-vis* a supranational EC. Dafydd Elis Thomas, the Plaid Cymru MP, has suggested rather mischievously that we are moving into an era of post-nationalism:[10] 'Sovereignty would not rest in any one spot. Europe would become an amorphous body with links and inter-action between regions, districts, cities and organisations.' This has attractions as a European equivalent of the global village. But it ignores the restrictions of geography and the power of history. For all but an élite minority, people's patterns of interaction remain very geograhically limited. On a few occasions in their lives they may travel some distance but there is now little prospect as there seemed to be in the sixties of a future in which distance travel would be almost routine. We now know that any significant expansion of that travel is environmentally costly. The expansion of telecommunica-tions can impart more information and images but not much more genuine interaction. The more remote the centres of decision-making become, the more they become the preserve of the professional lobbyist and the highly specialist politician. The case for maintaining substantial political power at levels where there is geographical coherence and accessibility is a strong one. It is the basis of the case for more power for the island communities.

But if the relevance of geography is still strong, the power of history is even stronger. Long periods of centralist rationalisation, long periods of political-economic divisions have proved to be remarkably flimsy in altering the orientation of people's identity, as the two Germanies and many of the Soviet states have illustrated. The complexity and subtlety of the process of inter-generational transmission of identity has been generally underestimated and under-researched by the social sciences. Too often it has been perceived as a very marginal influence in comparison with the really important trends of global cultural convergence. National identity has often been regarded as principally a time-lag factor. We now see widespread evidence of the vitality of national identity and, in particular, of its political manifestation. Statehood is perceived as an important aspect of that nationalism, whether involving merger as in Germany and Moldavia, or separation as in the Baltic states. The attraction of statehood where that coincides with a spontaneous rather than a manufactured national identity, is still powerful. It is powerful precisely because it offers a coming together of the spontaneous and the formal identity. That now much derided term 'national sovereignty' is what many peoples appear to want because it represents a readily understandable source of moral-political authority. It obviously does not mean that you determine the situation you find yourself in; it does mean that you have the ultimate right to make the choices in the context of that situation. Providing that national sovereignty rests on a genuinely democratic authority, it is hard to better it as the basis on which to continue to build international relations. Because it continues to have these great attractions of combining identity, political authority, and usually geographical coherence, the obituaries for the nation-state are somewhat premature. The nation-state as a geo-political concept has probably much vigour and a fair number of revivals still to go.

What is increasingly vulnerable is the state that is not reinforced by socio-cultural identity. The United Kingdom to some extent comes into that category, certainly as far as Scotland is concerned and probably Wales as well. The assumption that there is some kind of natural progression towards a combination of supra-nationalism and localism is probably a misinterpretation of diverse factors. Yes there are pressures towards supranationalism but what happens to the nation-states may depend more on the coherence of their identity than on their size. There may very well be serious pressures by the end of the decade from those viable nation-states to regain more of the powers they are in the process of losing, especially those states which do not feel they are dominant in the central decision-making processes. This is the trend we are seeing in the Soviet Union.

The notion of transnationalism rather than internationalism has certainly been with us before in imperialism, in strands of liberalism and Marxism. The prediction that 'new international entities would replace the nation-state'[11] was plausible in its period. But politicised ethnicity with the nation-state as its focus has proved remarkably robust. The problem which many have is in coming to terms with the different faces of that ethnicity – a positive reinforcement of social solidarity or the basis of an aggressive exclusiveness. To attempt to replace and supersede that sense of communal identity is probably futile because it fails to understand basic characteristics of human society, the need for attachment and for social identity, and the need to operate in recognisable structures which express this. The notion that by altering institutions you can readily alter the basis of ethnic identification is dubious. The problem is how best do you accommodate it as a positive force. Where you have a misalignment of political power and ethnicity, you have a potentially unstable situation. There are various ways in which it may resolve itself, but the underlying tensions may have surprising tenacity.

If we recognise the problems of political power and ethnic identity and also the importance of securing a democracy which is accessible and is not the exclusive preserve of the professional lobbyist, the bureaucrat and the career politician, what are the implications for the desirable direction of change in Europe and Scotland's place in it? There is an outstanding need for international institutions covering all of Europe to provide an orderly and structured way of dealing with conflict and rights and of securing environmental and economic co-operation. But there is also a need to oppose those trends in European institutions which markedly increase centralised power at the expense of national and local democracy. So the European dimension offers Scotland positive opportunities but also many problems. If it is seen primarily as a means of influencing decisions in the EC, there is no clear-cut advantage between independence and a domestic legislature. Under certain political circumstances the balance-sheet might be fairly even. If there is a more innovative approach to Scotland's relationships in Europe, then the independence case is strengthened. But either way, Europe offers no escape from the priority of seeking a negotiated settlement with other parts of the UK and one which can gain a wide range of support in Scotland. Whatever the ultimate constitutional status that Scotland attains, Europe will be an arena of problems as well as opportunities but not the source of easy solutions.

7

The SNP and the Scottish Working Class

TOM GALLAGHER

Working-class Scots belong to the social category C2 (skilled manual) or DE (semi/unskilled manual, unemployed). Multinational companies or else the local authority or UK-based public sector employs the bulk of the labour force belonging to these social categories. However, through the 1980s unemployment rates of 30-40% were not uncommon in some of Labour's safest Scottish seats. If employed, most earn wages below the UK average income; many may have a direct experience of poverty or want. Ordinary Scots such as these have a more passionate interest in football, TV soap operas, or the latest pop music trends than they do in politics; tabloid newspapers are their favourite reading matter. They are more likely to be council tenants than owner-occupiers, more likely to depend on public transport than to own a car. Unusually high incidences of lung cancer and heart disease among those in social category DE are testimony to an unhealthy lifestyle which may perhaps reveal an unduly fatalistic attitude to life. They are people whose voices are seldom raised in the political arena or listened to with any consistency: their silence does not cause the leadership of the party that they normally support any loss of sleep. To those with no commitment to the established political order, the Scottish working class is a sleeping political giant, but it is one that has obstinately refused to waken up and flex its collective muscles, however often it may have stirred in its sleep.

It was in the 1960s that the SNP first began to receive support from large numbers of working-class voters. Municipal elections in the larger urban conurbations between 1967 and 1969 demonstrated the party's new-found appeal to voters hitherto almost unaware of its existence. The SNP lacked a strategy for local government and many of its councillors proved to be quite inexperienced in municipal affairs. Those standing in Labour seats who had never expected political responsibility to be thrust upon them, at least so quickly, benefited from the sharp unpopularity of the Labour government. Local grievances concerning the management of council housing, the upheavals brought about by unimaginative redevelopment programmes, and occasional corruption scandals which were blamed on Labour (or which the party was seen as too ineffectual to solve, as in a city like Edinburgh where it had long been in opposition) accelerated the swing to the SNP.

Those with relatively weak attachments to the main parties had fewest qualms about supporting an unknown force like the SNP.[1] In the 1960s changes in the social structure of Scotland were influencing political behaviour which had not registered any big fluctuations since possibly as far back as the early 1930s. Industrial decline was robbing the Conservatives of the support they had long enjoyed in the working class, especially among skilled workers.[2] As recently as the 1955 General Election (when even a Clydeside seat like Govan returned a Tory), the support of many skilled manual workers enabled the Tories to emerge as Scotland's largest party. Further erosion in support resulted as the religious polarisation which had divided part of the working class into Protestant and Catholic segments, declined as a significant political variable thanks to the growth of intermarriage and vastly improved inter-church relations.[3] Especially among the young, a Tory appeal based on Protestant solidarity or allegiance to the union, or else to the more nebulous concept of local patriotism, cut little ice. The British imperial state which these symbols evoked was passing into history; the pace of social change locally also made them seem increasingly archaic.

The move to peripheral housing schemes or (in the case of the more upwardly mobile) to new towns like Cumbernauld or East Kilbride, broke down old patterns of close-knit working-class community living. There were swift political repercussions as shown by the emergence of the SNP as the largest party when the local authority for Cumbernauld held its first election in 1968. Young families susceptible to new political appeals after having shaken off the dust of old neighbourhoods, predominated in the new towns. The SNP in the 1960s appealed strongly to the young who comprised a very large part of its active membership.[4] It also appealed to previous non-voters within the working class whose patriotism had rested at the football level until tapped by SNP propaganda.[5] But even in the politically free-flowing 1960s the party was unable to make Scottishness a new focal point in politics, vying with class as a determinant of political behaviour. In a literate country like Scotland where a large circulation socialist weekly, *Forward,* was sustained for half a century, the Nationalist failure to establish a weekly or even monthly counterpart was significant. So was the lack of success in creating political festivals or symbolic occasions that could be a rallying-point for deepening the party's influence beyond the electoral arena or its own core following.

In 1989, the SNP chairman's 'sound-bite' in his conference address concerned Radio Free Scotland, a pirate radio transmitter which he had operated in the 1960s. Stung by the BBC's failure to broadcast live his speech,[6] Mr Wilson asserted that 'were I still controller . . . and still had the equipment, I would willingly author-ise the jamming of this unremitting English propaganda'.[7] The chances are that very few Scots would have had any recollections of Radio Free Scotland. Scottish identity in the political sense had been too ill-defined for such an initiative to capture the imagination of a broad audience.

In the 1970s the SNP was to be given an even stronger platform from which to break the Anglo-Scottish constitutional mould thanks to the parliamentary breakthrough that it enjoyed in 1974. Memories of its inglorious 1960s forays into local politics were forgotten as British economic failure and growing political discord revealed a malaise at the heart of the state. The simultaneous discovery of huge oil deposits off the Scottish coast sharpened discontent as the SNP argued that a Scottish leap forward into a viable economic future outside the ailing British state was at hand. For a few years in the mid-1970s, political independence looked less like a romantic pipe-dream than at any other time before or since. But the SNP was no more successful in politicising society in a nationalist direction than it had been in the 1960s. The perceived need to concentrate so much energy upon Westminster, whose devious ways the party was oblivious of, led to this task being overlooked. Running second to Labour in most of its seats, the SNP was unlucky that Scotland went nearly four years without a by-election, one of which could quite easily have precipitated a general election . . . and that longed for breakthrough in Labour strongholds.

In 1978, when by-elections followed in rapid succession in two working-class seats (Glasgow Garscadden and Hamilton, as well as in more socially-mixed Berwick and East Lothian), they were easily held by Labour. The SNP's target working-class voters had grown cautious and defensive in the intervening period. The party's rather weak Westminster performance during the various devolution debates was probably of little account since the working class had shown no appetite for following constitutional debates even before they entered the turgid but crucial parliamentary stage. More significant was the continued UK economic downturn which the manufacturing sector continued to take the brunt of.

Between 1974 and 1985 Scotland was to lose one-third of its manufacturing labour force.[8] The example of the inter-war period showed how recession breeds resignation and not defiant radicalism among the working class and, even with the existence of oil wealth offering a potentially better future, pessimism narrowed working-class horizons as the 1970s wore on.

Despite having entered the iconography of Scottish labour history, the famous work-in at Upper Clyde Shipbuilders in 1971 proved to be a one-off event, more effective as an exercise in propaganda than as a success for workers' control. It was not to be a reliable guide to the mood of Scottish workers in the recessionary 1970s. The takeover by a workers' co-operative of the Beaverbrook printing plant in Glasgow after the move south to Manchester of the *Scottish Daily Express*, proved to be a depressing flop.[9] Jimmy Reid, the joint leader of the first sit-in, was lionised as a working-class hero but he was rejected in 1974 by the voters of Clydebank in favour of an uninspiring but no doubt reliable Labour worthy. (Before becoming a full-time journalist the only electoral success Reid enjoyed was at Glasgow University whose students elected him their rector in 1972.)

Reid was a Communist but working-class Scots were similarly unmoved when Jim Sillars, a more mainstream figure, Labour MP for South Ayrshire, and of whom, like Reid, great things had been expected, sought their support upon forming the breakaway Scottish Labour Party in 1976. It attracted 900 members, about one-quarter of the membership of the party he had left, who were heavily drawn from the ranks of journalists and the far-Left.[10] Lacking support from the unions or what there was of the community-based Left, it quickly imploded in the midst of power-struggles between its founder and 'entryists' supposedly intent on hijacking it.[11]

Even if such a disastrous launch had been avoided and a stable party with a coherent membership established, it is doubtful if the SLP could have carved out a secure working-class niche. The signs that would have indicated a working class that was increasingly politicised, were absent after 1974. A comprehensive survey carried out in the 1970s, examining the relationship between national consciousness and voting, found that Scottish identity had a low priority among Scottish voters as a source for political action; this was true even of SNP voters, only 13% of whom considered Scottish-English conflict to be fairly or very serious compared to a 62% rating for trade union/employer conflict.[12] Interestingly, 29% of all voters in the sample believed there was fairly or very serious conflict between Catholics and Protestants.[13]

A working class still troubled by ancestral quarrels which were fuelling an undeclared civil war in nearby Ulster, and whose material prospects were threatened by accelerating economic decline, proved impossible to detach from its Labour loyalties in the 1970s. It is worth recalling that Labour had still obtained forty Scottish seats in February 1974 and actually gained one in the October election, the SNP's high-point. The structure of a Scottish economy in which working-class jobs depended on high levels of foreign investment and higher levels of public spending than in the rest of the UK, may have created a culture of dependency resistant to the nationalist project which could easily be depicted as entailing a great deal of risk and uncertainty. In the absence of an indigenous Scottish manufacturing élite, much of the workforce had grown accustomed to decisions that determined whether or not they had a job being made by politicians or corporate executives in London or further afield. Skilled workers employed by multi-national companies, or semi- or unskilled workers employed by the large newly created local authorities, had little cause to view the Scottish dimension as being relevant to their immediate requirements. To Nationalist politicians who insisted that an oil-rich Scotland could banish the spectre of unemployment and lay-offs for the rest of their lifetimes, the average working-class voter was sceptical. It involved too great an imaginative leap, too much of a break with existing arrangements whereby employment had been generated from elsewhere, and therefore it was fraught with unacceptable uncertainty.

Scotland's ignominious exit from the World Cup in June 1978 may also have been a final blow to faith in Scottish capabilities, given the crucial importance of football for sustaining a sense of patriotism within the Scottish working class.

As the Labour Party moved into opposition in 1979 and ceased to be part of the governing establishment in London, it, and not the SNP, became the home for the majority of the discontented. The defeat of the last and the greatest of the urban Tory populists in 1979 revealed how the previous fifteen years were notable not so much for the rise of nationalism but for the consolidation of class-based politics: Teddy Taylor's loss of the seat which included Castlemilk, the largest public housing scheme in Europe, marked the end of one era and the beginning of another.

The split in Labour Party ranks produced by the emergence of the SDP in 1981 did not endanger its ascendancy. The C1s, clerical and office staff, who became an increasingly influential social group as the local state expanded in the 1960s and 1970s, comprised much of the SDP's support in the 1983 election. They are not a group that the SNP has had much success in appealing to, many being recruited from across the UK labour market. Increasingly they have identified with Labour because of its defence of a public sector threatened by government privatisation policies; they are comfortable with a party whose local high-flyers are increasingly drawn from the world of local administration. The attachment of the public sector white-collar salariat has given Labour a commanding lead in Scotland: in Strathclyde, as early as 1983, Labour was polling 8% better than would be predicted from the social structure of the region.[14] Since then the planning and investment strategies of Strathclyde have drawn the ruling Labour administration even closer to the C1s. Ambitious motorway plans, combined with the regeneration of the urban centre have occurred as disadvantage has increased out in the peripheral housing schemes containing the bulk of Glasgow's unskilled working-class voters. One much-publicised academic study detailed how the urban transformation making Glasgow a headline-grabbing city in 1990, was clearly a result of planning policies which discriminated against the rundown periphery.[15] But there have been few repercussions: Pat Lally, leader of Glasgow District Council and an architect of this strategy, represents undisturbed, a Castlemilk ward that clearly came out second-best from this approach.

The Militant tendency has been more to the fore than the SNP in tapping the alienation of those at the margins of society in both geographical and income terms. Before the anti-poll-tax campaign, the last time the SNP specifically targeted the working class was in the early 1980s when the 79 Group faction, campaigning for the party to become a fully-fledged socialist one, argued that this was the best way of weakening Labour's grip on the working class. The episode left a more lasting effect on the SNP which was plunged into shortlived but damaging internal turmoil than on its intended target.

However disappointing for some, the most numerous sector of the working class, the semi- or unskilled manual workers located in social category DE, have not swung in a radical direction as their living standards have been squeezed in the 1980s. Indeed political radicalism has not been a distinguishing feature of their political behaviour since their enfranchisement, participating in radical initiatives having found greater appeal with skilled workers and the lower middle class.

The picture for the rest of Europe suggests that Scotland is not at all unusual in this respect. In none of the countries that witnessed serious public agitation during the 1989 downfall of communism in eastern Europe did workers take a prominent initial role in events. Students, middle-class intellectuals, or religious activists comprised the risen people in Prague, Leipzig, and Timisoara. Elsewhere in Europe it is these groups that have shaped the radical agenda of the new politics based on concern for the environment, regional consciousness, or grassroots citizens' initiatives. It is students who have comprised some of the largest audiences for Jim Sillars and it was the students of Glasgow University who shook off their hedonism in 1990 to elect as their rector, Pat Kane, a highly gifted contemporary musician and writer.

So a decisive electoral breakthrough continues to elude the SNP because of its failure to win the confidence of significant numbers of working-class votes in Scotland's central belt for anything but a short period of time. This is the largest voting bloc in Scotland and if the SNP hopes to achieve self-government on its own terms it needs to effectively challenge the Labour Party's domination of the urban working-class electorate. A statement like that made by Gordon Wilson in 1986 unintentionally reveals how much of a passive observer the SNP has been, unable to sway working-class loyalties and not even sure of the forces at work in determining their electoral preferences:

> Every now and again the pressure builds up for change, ebbs a
> bit and then comes back stronger than ever. In 1979 the
> Westminster institutions, the Establishment, played for time
> successfully and the issue [self-government] lost ground among
> the Scottish electorate. From then on we seemed to go into a
> 'British' phase. Now we're coming out of that, and people are
> once more looking for Scottish solutions.[16]

In the absence of a coherent, long-term strategy to oust Labour from its strongholds, it is possible to observe a number of approaches regularly used by the SNP in order to boost its credibility in the main target areas.

On the positive side, the party has long realised that a high standard of representation can overcome the disadvantages that have long prevented it doing well in the urban belt. Attention to the needs of a local community is often not a strong point of Labour representatives who may have grown complacent after years of runaway victories. Where the SNP is more adapt at community politics than its chief rival, it means that the traditional Labour charges of being 'tartan Tories' or 'impractical dreamers' carry less force: the chances then arise of building a real SNP presence in local communities.

Gordon Wilson's ability to hold the largely working-class seat of Dundee East in four general elections (1974-87) arguably rested more on his ability to be a diligent constituency member than on that particular group of voters' receptivity to the nationalist message. In November 1988 Jim Sillars's breakthrough in Govan in large stemmed from his image as an energetic campaigner who offered a lifeline to a particularly hard-pressed inner-city constituency. His appeal was very much an individual one given that he is such a singular character who embodies seemingly contradictory features: a politician with strong traces of his working-class background who has not departed from his roots and who displays practical knowledge of how 'things are done', how the powerful exercise their sway. Since competence in the Scottish political context has long been associated with quietly modulated middle-class performers such as John Smith and Robin Cook, the emergence of this Scottish Bevan was bound to be widely noticed since it went so totally against the grain. But it was a time when the Thatcher juggernaut was sweeping all before it, when the proven and the familiar seemed inadequate to the task in front of them. Perhaps voting for a self-educated working-class populist evoked, in the minds of older voters, memories of a more achieving past since political heroes in Scotland seemed very much part of a bygone age. Afterwards SNP strategists came to see this victory more as a direct endorsement for their bold 'independence in Europe plans', which thus enabled them to spurn cross-party initiatives in favour of an uncompromising approach – without further gains being yielded.

Thanks to his presence in the constituency, Jim Sillars is already much better known to Govan voters than the previous MP who had held the seat (through various boundary changes) for nearly thirty years. But Sillars has much less chance of holding the seat than his uninspiring predecessor and will certainly not chalk up the huge majority which made Govan one of the safest Labour seats in Britain because the political culture of Clydeside still remains firmly Labourist.

Disappointment at Labour's dismal record locally and at Westminster helped engineer a sensational by-election triumph for an outside force. But Labour will only be in real political trouble on Clydeside if voters can be persuaded of the existence of a reliable alternative that will better serve their interests. In Govan, Sillars hopes to foster that perception so that, in the 1990s, voters will re-elect him and thus make him the first SNP MP to be returned for a Glasgow seat at a general election. To show that Govan was more than a by-election surprise, he has gone to greater lengths than would be necessary for most MPs in order to make himself accessible to ordinary voters and deal with their problems. A full-time office which consumes the MP's parliamentary allowance and much of his external income is his means of staying in touch with the grassroots while attending to other duties that devolve upon him as the SNP's best-known public figure.[17] Such a commitment has enabled him to take up the issue of drug-related crime, one of the main concerns in this inner-city area, especially of the elderly, and to ensure that bringing it under control becomes more of a police priority.[18]

The approach, costly in time and resources, may preserve Sillars's standing as a concerned man of the people even if his party fails to engineer another quick revival. (In the 1990 Scottish regional elections, the SNP did significantly better in three of the four wards making up the Govan parliamentary seat than anywhere else in the Strathclyde Region: it won 36.55% of the vote compared to 51.54% for Labour, a very creditable result given the SNP's utter failure to capitalise on the poll-tax in any other Scottish labour strongholds.)

The SNP can be forgiven for feeling rueful that it has to go to such lengths in order to appeal to voters slow to change their habits, but it is a hard road many challengers have to take in order to supplant a once-radical party still able to exploit an earlier record of achievement and struggle.

In SNP eyes, the Labour Party has been able to hang on because it has 'demobilised and depoliticised the people of Scotland'.[19] But there is not much evidence that the SNP has tried to counter this trend by quickening the pace of political debate during the long periods between elections. Political education work designed to improve the calibre of activists has often been neglected, if not completely ignored. The party showed little relish for engaging in public debate in early 1989 at a time when the formation of the Constitutional Convention and the introduction of the poll-tax had quickened the pace of politics and when, arguably, much misunderstanding about its reasons for rejecting the former needed to be dispelled. At a time when dedicated football fans are able to produce very professional magazines about their clubs from meagre resources, it is curious that the SNP lacks an official magazine or newspaper through which it can reach out to the wider public.

The nearest equivalent is the *Scots Independent*, a monthly newspaper with no official status, produced by those identified with the party's fundamentalist ('independence nothing less') wing. Its parochial style and its tendency to see the SNP as the natural home of all true Scots make it an embarrassment for more outward looking activists. Yet no alternative has been forthcoming even though, thanks to a few dedicated sellers who cover many of Glasgow's pubs, its embattled message is the only one that a lot of ordinary folk ever receive from the SNP.

That was until Jim Sillars began to write a regular weekly column in the Scottish edition of the *Sun* newspaper under the heading 'Big Jim Gives It To You Straight'. Especially during election periods, it is less a means to put over a positive image of the SNP more a vehicle for slamming political rivals for self-serving behaviour damaging to Scotland. Sillars does not think that there is anything unprincipled or opportunistic in writing for a paper which, in England, has been the flagship of Thatcherite values: '700,000 working-class Scots read the *Sun*. I would like their votes for us.'[20]

The SNP's preference for simple eye-catching slogans as a means of getting its message across may explain why Sillars finds the *Sun* such an effective medium and why a party quick to condemn others for 'the Englishing of Scotland' had greeted this improbable tie-up with silence.

More often than not, the party has appealed to the emotions of Scots rather than to their reason or even their materialist self-interest. Stark, even apocalyptic predictions about what the Scottish future will be if the SNP message falls on deaf ears, are staple fare. This shock therapy is probably designed to rouse ordinary Scots from their complacency but it may have the unintended effect of deepening their sense of helplessness or even despair. This was certainly my reaction as I heard Alex Salmond, MP, repeatedly warn at the 1989 SNP conference that 'there is no constitutional settlement short of full independence that can save our people or our country'.

However serious may be the economic and demographic challenges that lie ahead, the use of such lurid language and the neglect of sustained propaganda raises doubts about whether the party is serious about banishing depoliticisation. Past opportunistic behaviour and inflated claims about likely successes raise doubts about whether an aware and critical electorate is any more in the interest of the SNP than its political rivals.

Within the party, increasing emphasis has been placed on maintaining a united front in order to appear convincing to the wider electorate. This trend dates back to 1982 when serious Left-Right disagreements led to factions being proscribed. Although the SNP has since avoided the upheavals which have damaged the Labour Party and laid low the radical centre, this stress on uniformity has hampered the flow of ideas and arguments within the party and increased its dullness. It was used to muzzle many of the activists unhappy with the precipitate withdrawal from the Convention. Those who persisted in voicing their dissent were virtually accused of doing the work of the unionist enemy for them at a traumatic meeting of the National Council which ratified the withdrawal on 14 February, 1989.[21] At the same gathering, prominent figures savaged Scottish press outlets which only a few months before had been giving favourable coverage to the Govan breakthrough, for distorting the party's stance on independence in Europe and the Convention. The insecurity was well conveyed in a speech delivered by Margaret Ewing MP at the 1989 conference of the SNP:

The SNP's enemies had tried to divide them and create 1970s-

type splits but . . . faced by the unity of purpose that now
dominated the SNP . . . there had been a total failure to achieve
the clear goal of internal dissent.[22]

These words conjure up the image of a closed, almost tribal society
whose members have to draw close in face of the enemies conspiring
against them. To open-minded voters disillusioned with the ortho-
doxies and smug certainty of the two main parties, it is unlikely to
represent an appealing image. While insisting on such uniformity,
the SNP forgets that argument and dissent have been more accepted
in Scottish than in English political life, especially when alternative
courses of action or sets of principles, each possessing some merit,
are under consideration. Its image of a Scottish electorate impatient
of argument and ready to punish a party that practises vigorous open
debate, has more grounds in English than in Scottish reality; perhaps
because England's great power status required authoritative
government, the populace there has always been more comfortable
with a party that kept argument to a minimum and got on with the
business of governing.

Given the readiness with which internal differences of opinion are
seen as betraying weakness, the SNP is susceptible to the appeal of a
strong leader who has the authority to paper over the cracks of
disunity and has answers to the problems besetting the party. For a
while after Govan, Jim Sillars has assumed the mantle of de facto
leader. At the conference rostrum in 1989 his manner was that of a
stern Old Testament prophet exhorting a flock that can all too easily
be led astray to stick to the narrow but correct path. He is one of the
few politicians who can be guaranteed a large and attentive student
audience but, within the party, some younger activists criticise the
imperious style and the way that 'a branch meeting with Sillars
speaking can so easily turn into an audience with the Pope,
something that is deliberately encouraged'.[23] The public admission
of rising party star, Kenny McAskill, that it was Sillars's decision to
join the party that 'made it possible for people such as myself to feel
comfortable with the SNP' attests to his influence. 'If it was good
enough for him, it was good enough for us.'[24] Hitherto nobody quite
like Jim Sillars has burst to the front of Scottish politics. But in a
country where the masses have not hankered after charismatic
leaders in the way that the English sometimes have, it remains to be
seen whether such charisma can be translated into political staying
power.

Another means by which the SNP tries to get across to working-
-class voters is to brand its opponents not merely as rivals but as 'the
enemy'. It is no coincidence that in April 1989 Jim Sillars chose the
Glasgow housing scheme of Castlemilk to make a speech in which

Donald Dewar was branded an 'Uncle Tom' for allegedly betraying the interests of ordinary Scots by his ultra-cautious approach at Westminster. Such abrasive language is nothing new, it was only the dramatic metaphor that guaranteed it plenty of column inches in next day's press. Elements in the Labour old guard were able to respond in kind. Indeed it may be that the SNP feels it has a stake in the revival of the old guard since it gives effect to the charge that 'Labour is unionist to the core'.[25] The other face of the Labour Party, embodied in Scottish Labour Action, the radical pressure group for constitutional reform, disturbs its cosy world by showing that it is possible to be strongly nationally-minded while remaining in the Labour Party. Any success by the SLA in devolving party power from London to Scotland or in gaining conference approval for a dual mandate so that the party in Scotland is not immobilised by a fourth defeat in England, is bad news for SNP fundamentalism since it shows that there are other paths to freedom. By emphasising that the gulf between Labour and the SNP is unbridgeable, there is also more chance of ending the curious anomaly whereby a rather higher percentage of mainly lower-income Scots are prepared to support independence than normally vote for the SNP.

The Labour Party is the unofficial establishment in Scotland despite having been out of power centrally for over a decade; accordingly, the SNP has been able to highlight cases where its representatives have behaved in the manner of establishments everywhere. Indeed, exposing Labour chicanery is a key SNP priority and at a time when hard-hitting government policies such as the poll-tax are making ordinary people cast a more critical eye at the calibre of Labour representation, it looks as if the SNP barrage might have had some effect. But there is one snag: where a party denounces a rival for abandoning its supporters, as over the poll-tax, and offers a radical, principled alternative, the onus is clearly upon it not to deviate from the high standards it has set. Zealots have to be purer than pragmatists in order to retain their credibility which is something the SNP has discovered to its cost when councillors taking part in the non-payment campaign are discovered to have paid up; or when SNP councillors on Tayside vote to make local authority cleaners redundant at a time when Labour's feeble response to the privatisation of ancillary welfare services was supposedly one of the SNP's trump cards in the 1989 Glasgow Central by-election. The trouble with the SNP is that it is even more a coalition of different social interests than the Labour Party so that prescribing a code of collective morality upon which broad agreement can be found is no easy task.

Less risks are entailed when the SNP identifies itself with pres-

tigious popular movements abroad which have dethroned unrepresentative power holders in the name of the people. In 1989 Alex
Salmond was not alone in urging that 'people must see the SNP as
agents for change along the lines of Poland's Solidarity'.[26] But for
this to be possible the party would have to go beyond being a force
which is only visible to large numbers during the short weeks of an
election campaign; it would need to sink deeper roots in the
community and understand the forces at work in the educational
sphere and in the workplace that have conditioned the response of
the Scottish voters to the political challenges placed before them. In
the absence of the persecution experienced by Solidarity or of the
need to defend a widely spoken but endangered indigenous
language, this isn't easy. But it is not impossible as the mainstream
Basque Nationalist Party, the PNV, showed earlier this century.

The Partido Nacional Vasco built community centres and
promoted Basque sporting and cultural initiatives. The PNV 'was a
club offering the benefits of mutual support to its members'.[27] As a
result it was one of the few parties in Spain able to continue functioning (albeit clandestinely) under the Franco dictatorship; one
wonders if there would be much trace left of the SNP following a
similar clampdown in Scotland.

It is encouraging to see how the Young Student Nationalists (YSN)
are trying to extend the party's relevance beyond the electoral sphere
by campaigning actively about the plight of young Scots whether
they be homeless or working dangerous unsocial hours for low rates
of pay. In 1989, its success in overturning SNP conference pro-
cedures to ensure a discussion of the European Youth Charter, a
document addressing the implications of the Single European Act for
all young Europeans, is a sign that the importance of engaging in
practical solidarity rather than merely coining slogans about it may
be appreciated in the party.

The active marketing of the 'Independence in Europe' concept has
been designed to win round those Scots who fear being isolated in a
self-governing Scotland. This fear seems to be a real one in many
working-class communities where it is common for many family
members to reside outside Scotland. But absent has been an attempt
to make common cause with groups in other parts of Britain trying
to break free from an increasingly centralised and undemocratic
state.

Until the launching of Charter 88, there was little to latch on to: it
seeks nothing less than a democratic revolution to replace the archaic
and illiberal Westminster system with one that allows the citizens of
Britain in their respective countries and regions to participate in
decision-making as full citizens. Almost 10,000 people responded to

the Charter's manifesto in late 1988, but the SNP stayed aloof when it could have endorsed its emancipatory aims without going back on its independence commitment. It would have been a reassuring gesture for those Scots whose desire for self-government is qualified by the fear that it will cut them off from other communities in these islands with whom they have much in common. One wonders how many in the SNP are aware that the last time a west European country changed its constitution in the way that is planned for Scotland was in the mid-1970s when the democratic forces in Spain buried their rivalries and made common cause with liberal elements in the Franco regime in order to loosen the grip of authoritarianism. The triumph of democracy was not the work of any one party or individual but stemmed from a collective effort of the kind that, in embryo, Charter 88 may be the beginning of in this country.

This part of the discussion has mainly been concerned with the devices employed by the SNP in order to boost its influence among ordinary Scots, many of whom, it has to be said, are not politically motivated. On the positive side it identified the importance of high calibre political representatives while it found that the stress on party unity, on a simple message, on denouncing rivals as enemies, and on impulsively latching on to progressive causes elsewhere, had so far yielded meagre returns and may have damaged the party's standing.

HOW WORKING-CLASS SCOTS PERCEIVE THE SNP

After the 1989 European elections Jim Sillars expressed puzzlement that folk agree with every word he says but still go and vote for the Labour Party. He was referring to a credibility gap in which voters relate well to the emancipatory message transmitted by the party but stop short of translating this into steady electoral commitment. Is there something in the corporate image of the party that keeps ordinary voters at arm's length however much its policies relate to their needs? Certainly the ingrained habit of suggesting what is in the interests of the SNP is bound to be in the interests of the Scottish people can seem patronising, especially to Scots who desire change but are not as sure as their would-be liberators about what the way ahead should be. All parties are in the habit of insisting that their policies reflect not just the interests but also the underlying wishes of the electorate. But the SNP is supposed to be more than a party, more than a vote-gathering machine; it once projected itself as a movement out to liberate the Scottish people which, upon reaching the promised shore of independence, may well decide to disband, its task having been accomplished.

However, twenty years of campaigning in the political foreground have not given it an image or an appeal greatly different from that of the more class-based parties. No figure has emerged from the ranks of the SNP who has been able to carve out an appeal transcending party in the way that the former Plaid Cymru leader, Gwynfor Evans, managed to do in Wales. In 1979 his threat to fast till death unless the government honoured its promise to back a Welsh-language television station, was taken sufficiently seriously for the Thatcher government to make one of its few concessions to popular opposition sentiment. It is hard to envisage any nationalist in Scotland with the same cross-party stature being able to place the government in an equivalent dilemma.

Scots do not greatly respect the views or opinions of elected politicians. This was the finding of a 1987 System 3 poll which showed that even the views of newspaper columnists and television commentators were treated more seriously.[28] In its own behaviour, the party has been unable to counter the rather cynical view Scots have acquired about the ethical standards and motives of those who represent them.

Probably it is by its high-profile stance on the poll-tax that the SNP has endeavoured to most clearly improve its stock, especially with economically vulnerable sections of the community without the resources to meet the payments. In contrast to the cautious line of the Labour Party, the SNP has had no difficulty in espousing a policy of all-out resistance. During 1989, it signed up an army of non-payers as senior figures urged local residents in inner-city areas and housing schemes to defy the tax. By the close of the year, as non-payers began to be faced with court appearances, fines, and the possibility of warrant sales, concern was beginning to be expressed from within the party about the wisdom of its strategy. No back-up was being offered by party headquarters to local activists being asked by ordinary people who had responded to their campaign what they should do to stave off the sheriff's officer. Without practical means to shield people from the consequences of non-payment, the SNP was liable to be seriously damaged according to local activists sceptical about whether the resistance campaign had been seriously thought through. Such sceptics felt the campaign was badly flawed because it was conceived more from a desire to embarrass the Labour Party than to help those lower-income groups ground down by the poll-tax.

This miscalculation betrayed the middle-class character of the leadership – dominated as no other Scottish party is by members of the legal profession – eager to exploit the loopholes in the poll-tax legislation but out of touch with the conditions that the poorest sections of the population were living under. Some activists feared not only a loss of goodwill and trust if the SNP was seen to be cynically harnessing the anger of those on the margins of society, but also saw the danger that grassroots campaigners in working-class areas would grow disillusioned with the party, thus lessening its chances of breaking into Labour strongholds.

There is little evidence that the SNP benefits from the all-out attacks it regularly makes on the Labour Party. Concentrating on the shortcomings and duplicity of Labour probably does more to convince party members of the justice of their own cause than to make any impact on the wider electorate. At the Govan by-election, the SNP campaigners put aside the vendetta with Labour, perhaps aware that it was not the best way to court a normally rock-solid Labour constituency. But afterwards this blood-feud was resumed with a will as the SNP seized upon the possibility of delivering a knock-out blow to its chief competitor.

Such rivalry is part of the artificial world of party hype and division and it does not have much bearing on reality. There is much anecdotal evidence that the internecine warfare which is increasingly a Scottish political trademark, has an acutely disillusioning effect on ordinary voters and lowers their belief in the ability of politicians to change things. Polls have shown popular backing for electoral co-operation in the 1987 General Election, Scotland being the one area where tactical voting was widely practised in order to back whatever candidate stood the best chance of ousting a sitting Tory. The fact that the Tories lost over half their Scottish seats although their vote fell much less sharply, does not give their political rivals much food for thought. Electoral co-operation is firmly out and the SNP has even altered its constitution to make sure that a candidate is put up in every Scottish seat, the reasoning being that it must be a black day for Scotland if every voter is denied the chance of voting for 'Independence in Europe'.

These non-stop gladiatorial contests make a mockery of SNP claims (reiterated by Labour) that Scots are united in the face of Thatcherism. So long as sectarian rant infects the language of political exchange, it will undermine the view that Scots possess enough common ground and shared values to deserve recognition as a distinct community. A start could be made if, in winnable Tory seats, a truce was observed and a single opposition candidate stood, perhaps a consensual figure drawn from the ranks of education or the churches. It is doubtful if this would generate a revolt among voters suddenly starved of choice: it would more likely lead to a restoration of faith in politics as a means of finding concrete solutions for concrete problems.

Sterile two-party dogfights are a very British phenomenon and it is surprising that a party as European-minded as the SNP feels that it has nothing to learn from the consensual traditions of post-war European politics. Faced with a menace to liberty and future economic security in the shape of a continental Margaret Thatcher, reformist parties in countries like West Germany and the Benelux states would surely not hesitate before forming electoral pacts and doing all that was necessary to see off this menace. As the bipartisan approach of our continental neighbours becomes increasingly familiar to ordinary Scots, it is bound to reflect badly on the 'Independence in Europe' idea.

Is there an in-built tendency for Scottish progressives to fritter away their advantages by engaging in mindless sectarianism? During the inter-war years the Communist and Labour Parties behaved with similar blindness as they insisted to working-class voters that theirs was the only true path to freedom. The result was to discredit socialism among a generation of voters and to produce the machine politics that have served Scotland so ill.

The lesson of the 1980s is that if Scottish voters are faced with the choice of two gladiators in a quarrel that they don't have any appetite for, they'll go for the one they know – Labour. Winning the economic and political arguments but losing the electoral one often produces exasperation among the nationalists, causing them to preach to their target audience in almost self-righteous terms. Gordon Wilson was a past master of the style as party chairman, as his address to the conference in 1989 showed:

> Scottish independence is inevitable, but will only be ours when the Scottish people discard an outdated British identity in favour of relationships relevant to the twenty-first century.
>
> Scotland must be in the vanguard of countries moving towards democratic self-government as a new era of nationalism sweeps Europe.[29]

The ringing certainties contained in this statement evoke uneasy parallels with the style of a Prime Minister prone to see the world in similar black and white terms. It is doubtful if ordinary Scots are as confident about the future or wish to be in any political vanguard. By misreading their mood and lecturing to them, the SNP may be erecting an iron curtain between itself and those whom it wishes to influence.

Perhaps ordinary people who in their daily lives come up against the harsher side of the state have a more instinctive awareness of how desperately hard it will be to achieve independence and that they are the ones likely to pay dearly if the central state responds toughly to the challenge. SNP spokesmen who argue that independence is there for the taking and that a Prime Minister who can veto devolution will be unable to defy a demand for independence if it is made by a majority of Scots MPs, come across as naïve and very sheltered from the harsh realities of life. Between 1880 and 1918 self-government was denied to the Irish because they could not muster a majority in both Houses of Parliament and the imperial temper of Mrs Thatcher suggested that she would not be averse to imposing similar stiff conditions.

People in the west of Scotland are all too aware of the intractable conflict in neighbouring Ulster that owes a lot of its staying-power to British manipulation and intransigence. By contrast the SNP has done its best to ignore it and to insist that Scotland is different. Accordingly it makes no effort to address widely held subconscious fears about Scotland's unresolved communal tensions.

These Protestant-Catholic tensions are largely a working-class phenomenon and since they prevent working-class Scots from fully trusting one another, they may be impairing the level of self-confidence and mutual regard necessary for a successful drive towards self-government. This oversight once again raises doubts about whether the SNP is in touch with popular concerns and attitudes, surely a necessity for a party with such bold aims.

It is unclear whether anyone in the SNP has tried to work out why such residual loyalty to the Labour Party exists in the Scottish working class even though its record of service is unimpressive. The bafflement of even seasoned operators like Jim Sillars suggests that a gulf of perception exists. Less embattled younger student members are prepared to concede, as one put it to me, that 'in attacking Labour we alienate a lot of people whose families have been Labour all their lives: we have to accept that places exist where Labour has helped people in the past and where a debt of gratitude still exists'.

Such an honest appraisal might, in time, produce a more carefully thought-out strategy to coax working-class voters away from failed Labour solutions. This priority was far from the mind of Alex Salmond in November 1989 when, at a rally of young activists, he declared that 'it is only through undermining the Labour Party in Scotland that we can achieve our objectives'. He then went on to predict that 'in the event of another Labour defeat, the self-belief of Labour activists will be compromised beyond recovery'.[30]

Salmond failed to appreciate that the trench warfare favoured by the SNP postpones the realignment of Scottish politics necessary if his party is to make significant headway. Labour activists would not be human if the abuse coming from the SNP did not instil a grim determination not to give way before them even if no progress is made in dislodging their Tory foe from office. Nobody is recommending that the SNP stand down before Labour. Rather the emphasis needs to be on more imaginative tactics in which reason and common sense take over from a primitive desire for revenge (something that by his pronouncements on becoming leader in 1990 Salmond may be realising). When a more mature approach to coping with a stubborn rival becomes the norm, then it is surely likely that more working-class Scots will look to the domestic arena for salvation rather than placing their hopes in British solutions based on the south of England rejecting Thatcherism.

The SNP has not grasped the degree to which, when making political choices, ordinary Scots are influenced by events and trends in the rest of the UK. This was shown in mid-1989 when a clutch of polls revealed that Labour might just be electable in the south. It turned out that the large floating vote in the Glasgow Central by-election was more influenced by Labour's upturn in England than by the obviously appealing and well-packaged 'Independence in Europe' strategy of the SNP.

Nor do they appear to have grasped the extent to which their target working-class audience is influenced by the mainly London-based broadcasting media, by a myriad of human contacts south of the border, and by the fact that the Scottish public sector is recruited from the UK labour market. There are workers in the ancillary sector of the NHS and elsewhere who are aware, from their own everyday experiences, that in many respects Scotland is an economic colony but who are reluctant to speak in outright nationalist terms out of a desire not to alienate colleagues who hail from England.

THE CONSTITUTIONAL CONVENTION

However hard it may have tried the SNP has been unable to break down the implicit feeling harboured by many ordinary Scots that they simply do not have what it takes to control their own political future either because of internal divisions or owing to the power of the state currently ruling over them. No SNP-sponsored campaign of resistance to an unpopular and scarcely representative government has taken hold among those bearing the brunt of regressive economic and social policies; nor have they shown any desire to actively punish the Labour Party for failing to shield them from measures like the poll-tax. In response, an exasperated SNP has turned in on itself and, like a prophet spurned, has proclaimed with even greater insistence that it, and it alone, represents Scotland's true interests. This isolationist mood used to be a feature of the mainly rural-based fundamentalist wing of the SNP, but the response to the cross-party campaign for self-government in 1988-90 showed that it extended to many urban radicals – it was certainly reflected in the demeanour of those younger recruits drawn to the party after the Govan victory. Accordingly, Léft-Right differences grew increasingly meaningless as protagonists in earlier internal disputes sank their differences and rallied behind the clamorous slogan of 'Independence in Europe'.

So much emotional capital was sunk into persuading Scots that membership of the EC was an attainable goal that would guarantee economic viability and banish fear of isolation that, for its advocates, any other way forward was a ruse or a diversion. Opinion polls measured considerable approval for 'Independence in Europe' as a legitimate ideal but the preferred constitutional option remained a parliament for Scotland within the United Kingdom.

This was the goal of the Campaign for a Scottish Assembly which, since 1979, had been seeking to obtain cross-party agreement and the backing of major Scottish institutions behind a strategy to create a governing assembly more representative than the one presently controlling Scottish affairs. The aim was revolutionary since it saw sovereignty as located in the Scottish people not the Westminster Parliament, but the approach was a gradualist one. More emphasis was placed on gaining the adherence of influential strands of opinion such as the trade unions, the churches, local government, and the professions, than on building a mass movement.

Plenty of ordinary Scots remained unaware of its activities even after the issuing in July 1988 of a *Claim of Right for Scotland*. This was a document drawn up by two retired senior civil servants who had been at the heart of Scottish government for many decades in which the case was made for a new form of Scottish government that would not be under the jurisdiction of the existing Westminster system on matters crucial to Scotland's interest. The formation of a Constitutional Convention (hereafter CC) was deemed to be the most appropriate means to pressurise Westminster into recognising the strength of Scottish feeling and entering into negotiations for a new Anglo-Scottish settlement. Events thereafter moved quickly.

A business committee met on 28 January, 1989 and agreed that a 15-member Scottish Constitutional Convention should meet at the end of March to begin planning a structure of government for Scotland. On 30 March, 1989 the first meeting of the Convention took place in the Assembly Hall on the Mound in Edinburgh. The presence of the great majority of Scottish MPs and of foreign diplomats gave the event a considerable sense of occasion which was powerfully relayed in the speech of Canon Kenyon Wright. He left his audience in no doubt about the radical nature of the constitutional initiative when he asked:

> If we produce a detailed scheme which has the backing of Scotland's people, what happens if that other voice we all

know so well responds by saying: 'We say no and we are the state'? Well, we say yes and we are the people, and in the last analysis Scotland believes not in the 'Royal we' but in 'we the people'.[31]

Applauding this rousing end to his speech were most of Labour's forty-nine Scottish MPs. The party had swallowed grave doubts about identifying with an initiative which placed nationalism at the top of the agenda upon Scottish leader Donald Dewar being won round by the force of the arguments contained in the Claim of Right.

But absent from the Assembly Hall was the SNP whose leadership had spurned the CC in January 1989, the membership confirming the decision some weeks later through the SNP National Council. The main sticking point was the absence of plans for an early referendum in which the Scottish people would be asked to choose a preferred option for the constitutional future of their country. The party was unable, or else unwilling, to appreciate the legitimate difficulties in organising and financing what would be the equivalent of a general election for a body which had only emerged after long years of delicate negotiations and for which such a course might have proved destabilising. It seemed to discount the propaganda windfall likely to accrue to it, the party long identified in the public eye with the national cause, when such an array of representative Scots gave their blessing to a high-profile campaign couched in nationalist terms. Similarly, the possibilities, opened up by the CC of establishing common ground with trade unions and members of the professions, groups long courted by the SNP, failed to register. Instead of being a forum where converts could be made, rapport established, and credibility built up in the eyes of the Scottish electorate, the CC was dismissed by the SNP as a unionist talking shop because it did not put independence at the forefront of its agenda.

The Claim of Right had not ruled out independence or dismissed it as an aspiration unworthy of the Scots but had argued that a gradualist strategy should first be attempted to instil solidarity among the Scots and allow them to get used to co-operating behind a national purpose. Nor, as some SNP leaders alleged, did the CSA's thinking revolve around resurrecting the discredited 1978 Devolution Bill. Frequently it was made clear that a modern model of Scottish self-government was envisaged, one far removed from anything proposed in the 1970s.

The bitter conclusion of the 1978-9 devolution campaign had marked the SNP psychologically and it drew on its experiences then to judge the constitutional initiative taking place a decade later. Thus the Labour Party's involvement in the Convention was half-hearted and duplicitous because it was still the unionist party which, in the

1970s, had dangled a flawed devolution package before impression-able Scots in order to discredit the self-government cause. The party refused to acknowledge that many Labour activists now put their passion for internal self-government ahead of their desire to exercise power in London. The new mood was shown at the opening Convention meeting when Councillor Jean McFadden, treasurer of Glasgow District Council, after admitting that she had voted 'No' in 1979, declared that 'We want independence now'.[32]

The SNP's acrimonious spurning of the Convention was followed by a steady decline in its poll ratings. From being only 3% behind Labour in January 1989 it fell back to over twenty-five points behind as the first anniversary of Govan approached. The much anticipated gains in the June 1989 European Elections, thought by many to be behind the aggressive strategy of the party, did not materialise. A MORI poll in September 1989 showed that nearly as many SNP voters disagreed with the decision not to take part in the Convention unless certain conditions were met, as went along with the leader-ship: eloquent testimony of the party's failure to communicate with its own core electorate never mind the wider population.[33]

The only note of self-doubt (a very faint one) emanated from Alex Salmond in November 1989 when he stated that the party had erred in not explaining clearly enough its grounds for non-participation in the CC:

> the key sticking-point was the need to have a referendum, not the level of SNP membership permitted in the Convention, nor sovereignty, a concept people find difficult to understand. If we had explained that more clearly most Scots would have seen our point.[34]

In September 1990, the willingness of Strathclyde Regional Council leader, Charles Gray, to place his local authority's weight behind a referendum so as to test the popular verdict towards the Convention's strategy of self-government makes it clear that the door is still open for the SNP to return and make the Convention a forum for all the parties committed to self-government.

Younger members have been altogether more critical, albeit in private, given the hostility shown to dissenters on this matter. One argued that the announcement of withdrawal from the Convention made by Gordon Wilson on 30 January was 'a classic example of the leadership making the decision and to hell with the membership; it was shameful that it was by switching on their televisions at night that the party members first got to hear of it'. Another followed by arguing that 'parties organise their internal affairs along the lines they would wish to run their nation and that more needs to be done for the SNP to become comfortable with dissent'.[35]

If the SNP is really serious about wishing to bring about a realignment of Scottish politics, it might look again at a strategy which has brought it few of the electoral gains that it was hoping for. The insistence of some of its spokespersons that Scotland's future is secure in its hands alone is very counter-productive since it reminds many of the proprietorial attitude that the Tories have to the British state. If the Tories fundamentally alter their style in the post-Thatcher years and the SNP carries on with a self-righteous, hectoring approach not only to its opponents but to the voters, this would be a sure way to alienate its target vote. In the 1980s Scots have shown abundant proof that they are fed up with confrontational politics whether decked out in the Union Jack or the Scottish Saltire.

In the face of momentous events across eastern Europe where bureaucratic state tyrannies were toppled in large part thanks to the ability of disparate groups to unite, the SNP's behaviour appears even more parochial and self-centred – the very type of behaviour which in Eastern Europe before the last war, helped to weaken democratic forces and prepare the ground for despotism. The scenario is unlikely to unfold in Scotland but the SNP's policy is likely to increase the influence within the Labour Party of the most reactionary elements from the world of local government and the more hide-bound trade unions who fear offering more responsibility to people for their own affairs and who see the Convention as disrupting the comfortable routines that they have built up.

The Campaign for a Scottish Assembly, within whose ranks have assembled many non-sectarian SNPers, has shown that no party can claim a monopoly of patriotism. Two precious bequests to Scottish political life, the Convention and the Claim of Right, provide the means for a national constitutional movement to emerge to champion Scotland's right to self-determination. The fact that the SNP has spurned it for reasons that cut no ice with nearly half of its own voters, says little for its sense of political realism.

It is hopefully not too late for the party to reinvolve itself with the work of the Convention. In the words of Isobel Lindsay, national convener of the Campaign for a Scottish Assembly, its scheme for a Scottish Parliament gives Scotland at least 70% of powers that she would enjoy under any system of outright independence.[36] If the SNP were to reformulate its strategy and cease giving the impression that it possesses a monopoly of truth, the political rewards might start to flow its way sooner than many think from a public grateful at the sight of at least one party renouncing political cant.

Although I am not a member of the party, it has long been clear to me that the SNP has some of the most dedicated and selfless activists to be found in any branch of Scottish political life. The spoils of office and the rewards of electoral success have not been motivating factors for many of its members, especially since so few of them have come the way of the SNP. The leadership which, by the very nature of politics, contains ambitious and driven people, has borne this disappointment far less stoically. Its tendency to categorise voters who resist the independence message as being less than true Scots raises the danger that it will be trapped in an electoral ghetto. Indeed, however hotly they might deny it, the demeanour of some leaders leaves the unmistakable impression that they are content to represent a minority of 'true Scots' in the guise of a permanent oppositional force.

The future of the party and its relevance to the concerns of the people may well depend on whether younger and more outward-looking party members find the confidence to argue against the exclusive position the leadership got the party into during 1989-90. If not, the danger is that the SNP will become increasingly isolationist and embittered, leaving the way for the Labour Party to enjoy total sway in its working-class strongholds. One-party rule, whoever exercises it, clogs the arteries of politics and, as has been shown in the west of Scotland for much of the post-war period, offers an appalling service to the ordinary voter.

The tenor of this chapter would suggest that the realignment of politics is unlikely to start with the Scottish working class but its response is crucial for ensuring the removal of the Scottish political log-jam. If the SNP is serious about breaking down the existing party blocs, it could do well to debate the options open to it honestly and openly rather than insist on shrill displays of unity.

The appointment of a leader who has the skill and the confidence to take the debate into the opposition camp suggests that the siege mentality which has gripped the party for some time may be wearing off. A less embattled party that is no longer so preoccupied with denouncing its chief opponent and more willing to offer a convincing vision of what a new Scotland would be like under its direction, may find that the working-class fortresses it has tilted its lances against are not so impregnable after all.

8

The Scottish Middle Class and the National Debate

STEPHEN MAXWELL

There is a mystery about the Scottish middle class. In most liberal democracies the middle class has been not only the dominant social group but also the main source of national leadership. From its bases of power in the national institutions of government, law, education and the church, and in commerce, industry, finance and the media the middle class has provided the most sensitive register of the changing prospects of its national community and the directing force of the community's response.

Chief among its objectives have been the perpetuation of its own privilege and power at home and the extension of its prestige and power abroad. But in most countries the middle class has acted on the assumption that its own security and power depend on the strength and cohesion of the national community as a whole.

The Scottish middle class is an exception. In recent decades, as Scotland's circumstances have undergone rapid and dramatic change, the Scottish middle class has managed only a stuttering, hesitant and ineffectual response. In the last twenty years Scotland has emerged as the world's fifth largest producer of oil. She has suffered a massive takeover of her industrial assets. She has experienced a near doubling of the proportion of her people living in relative poverty. She has been subjected to a decade of radical government by a party which her voters have rejected with increasing insistence at three successive elections. More and more areas of her national life have been exposed to the impact of an accelerating pace of international integration. Yet in this period of tumultuous change the Scottish imagination has seemed unable to comprehend, let alone bridge, the growing gulf between Scotland's reality and Scotland's potential. Responsibility for that failure lies primarily on the shoulders of those groups in society which by privilege of education and advantage of position in the institutions which shape opinion and determine society's potential for collective action – that is to say, the middle classes.

The strength of the Labourist tradition and its attendant mythology in Scotland makes it necessary to insist – in a way which would be superfluous in any other Western country – on the fact of middle-class dominance. There are, it is true, statistical differences in the occupational structures of Scotland and of England and Wales, for example in the proportionate size of the professional, managerial and administrative groups and manual workers. But small differences of 2 or 3 % in the proportionate shares of different occupational groups do not make a difference between middle-class dominance and non-dominance. The long years of Labour's political dominance in Scotland has eroded the social dominance of the middle class only at the margins. People of middle-class education and family background dominate virtually every institution which possesses significant power: Scottish industry and finance, education, media, the law, central and local government, the political parties including the Labour Party, the churches, all are conspicuously 'bourgeois' in character. If it is a little less unusual in Scotland than in England to find someone of working-class background in a commanding position in, say, the media or education, the difference is of very modest degree and certainly far too little to explain the difference between the national roles of the middle class in Scotland and the middle classes in other Western countries.

If the Scottish middle class is peculiarly defective in its capacity for national leadership the implications for Scotland's future are grave. In 'post-industrial' society the dominance of the middle class looks set to increase. The decline of the manufacturing labour force has been even more rapid in Scotland than in most other industrialised societies. The non-manufacturing sections of the labour force are dispersed and difficult to organise. It is improbable that any distinctively working-class formation will be able to act as a determining force in the affairs of a Western democracy for the foreseeable future. The live issues in the politics of the twenty-first century are likely to reflect middle-class not working-class concerns. Of course the issues themselves – the environment, the centralisation of power, cultural autonomy in an age of mass communications, the relations between developed and developing countries – affect working-class people as much as middle-class people. But the ideological formulations of these problems, the terms in which they are debated, the organisational forms they inspire are likely to reflect middle-class values and skills. If Scotland is to define and negotiate her own interest in the 'post-industrial' world, the Scottish middle class will have to find a new will for public leadership.

The Scottish middle class is not being treated here in some sub-Marxist way as a cohesive economic interest with a predetermined role in Scotland's history. The term middle-class is used only to describe those members of society who make their living through utilising significant accumulated assets, whether in the form of education or training or financial capital. The only assumptions made – and then as elements of a working hypothesis – are that members of these middle-class groups, such as doctors, teachers, businessmen, administrators, and managers, have an interest in maximising the career opportunities available to themselves and to their children within their own community and that they recognise that their prospects depend crucially on the fortunes of the national community as a whole. No further assumption is made about a common middle-class interest. Indeed we shall see that in the 1980s London governments have attempted, with some success, to polarise the interests of middle-class groups in Scotland.

The failure of the Scottish middle class in recent decades can be illuminated, with appropriate caveats about the hazards of comparisons through time and across cultures, by comparisons both with Scotland's past and with the contemporary experience of other developed societies.

In the eighteenth and nineteenth centuries the Scottish middle class played a role of national leadership with considerable, if diminishing, energy. The Scottish Enlightenment represented an effort by Scottish intellectuals with their roots in Scotland's commercial, legal and church middle classes to liberate Scotland from religious obscurantism and establish her claim to membership of rational, enlightened Europe.

In the early nineteenth century Walter Scott, of impeccably bourgeois background, reacted to the English encroachment on Scottish institutions by promoting an image of historical Scotland even as the succeeding generation of Edinburgh lawyers represented by Cockburn was preparing a campaign to reform Scotland's political system after an English model, and sections of the West of Scotland middle classes were laying the foundations of Scotland's industrial pre-eminence.

In the mid-nineteenth century, when traditional Scottish institutions were clearly on the defensive, the Disruption of 1843 demonstrated the vigour with which one section of the Scottish middle class could defend Scottish tradition against the attacks of a meddling Westminster Parliament. By the mid-century the Scottish industrial middle class had established itself as one of the driving forces of Britain's imperial economy.

The erosion of the economic base of bourgeois Scotland which took place in the first half of the twentieth century did not drain Scotland's middle classes of all their vitality. The Independent Labour Party drew notably on middle-class leadership. Scots industrialists took a leading role in the rationalisation of British industry in the inter-war period as well as leading campaigns to restructure the Scottish economy. Boyd Orr and Walter Elliot confronted some of Scotland's social problems while contemporaries such as A. D. Lindsay, John Grierson and John Reith explored, in their very different styles, the implications of the new technologies of communication for the future of democracy in a mass society.

After the Second World War however, the springs of vitality began to dry up. As wartime Scottish Secretary, Tom Johnston, created an all-party Council of State through which to pursue nation-building initiatives such as the creation of the North of Scotland Hydro-Electric Board. But the momentum of Scottish reform did not survive into the 1950s. The limited but significant autonomy which Johnston enjoyed was lost in the programmes of British reform initiated by the post-war Labour government. While these reforms brought major benefits to the working-class people of Scotland they limited the opportunities for the exercise of public leadership from a Scottish base. Where the effort was made as with the Scottish Covenant for Home Rule it was on too narrow an ideological base and was quickly smothered by the exigencies of British politics. If Johnston left a legacy to the Scottish middle class lay in the re-inforcement of the belief that Scottish problems could be tackled most effectively through a state-sponsored consensus and in the founding of the corporate or sub-corporatist system of Scottish government.[1]

The 1960s witnessed the publication of a variety of diagnoses and prognoses of Scotland's social and economic problems: the Toothill report on economic development, the Oceanspan strategy, the Cullingworth report on Scotland's housing. But if there was anything approaching a coherent and sustained response it was found in the elaboration of regional development policies within a corporatist framework, supported by the vigorous promotional activities of the Scottish Council (Development and Industry). With hindsight the parameters of this response were too confined and parochial to allow an adequate response to the changes in Scotland's environment signalled by the United Kingdom's loss of international political and economic power.

It was in the 1970s however that the weakness of the Scottish middle class was most cruelly exposed. In spite of a conjunction of circumstances more favourable to Scotland's prospects for economic development and social progress than had obtained for many decades, the Scottish middle class produced only a mouse of a response.

For most of the twentieth century the weakness of the Scottish economy has provided the Scottish middle class with an alibi for inaction. The discovery at the very end of the 1960s of major reserves of oil off Scotland's coasts and the multiple rise in the world price of oil in 1973 blew that alibi away. The discoveries gave Scotland a potential for economic development greater than at any time since her economic 'take-off' in the eighteenth century on the basis of her coal and iron ore reserves. What is more the economic constraint on Scottish initiative was lifted at a time when the penalties for inaction were growing steadily more severe.

In 1960 the United Kingdom stood fourth in the world league of income per head. By the end of the 1970s she was struggling to hold a place in the top twenty. Scotland's unemployment was pointing sharply upwards for most of the seventies: the 100,000 mark was passed – for the first time since the war – in 1973 under the Conservative government of Edward Heath: the 200,000 mark was touched in 1978 under the succeeding Labour government. From 1973 a series of reports drew public attention to the revival of large-scale poverty in Scotland with claims that nearly one in five Scots was living in poverty or on its margins. Scotland's housing problems were exhaustively publicised. The role of foreign multi-national companies in developing the oil reserves heightened Scots' awareness of the high level of external ownership of their industrial assets as of the land itself. In the 1970s the opportunity for positive action and the need for radical change were in dramatic coincidence.

Elsewhere in the world, societies whose economic potential had been similarly transformed by the revaluation of natural resources were in a ferment of change. Developing countries such as Libya, Nigeria and Kuwait rushed to seize the development opportunities offered by the oil boom. So too did developed societies such as the Canadian provinces of Alberta and Quebec and Scotland's North Sea neighbour Norway.

In 1971 the thirty-year reign of the Social Credit Party in Alberta was brought to an end by the election of the Progressive Conservative Party. The Progressives were fired with an ambition to carry through an industrial revolution based on the local processing of Alberta's natural resources. Their vigorously interventionist policies produced a series of notable initiatives including the creation of the Alberta Energy Company, the purchase of Pacific Western Airlines, the creation of the Alberta Heritage Fund to secure a long-term income to the people of Alberta from the oil developments, the creation of an Albertan Energy Resources Conservation Board to control industrial development and the development by the Alberta Gas Trunk Company of plans for Albertan-controlled petrochemical projects. These institutional innovations were supported by no less radical interventions on oil prices and taxes. For a government of provincial businessmen ideologically hostile to state intervention this record was eloquent testimony to the energising impact of the world revolution in oil prices.

The impact was no less profound in Norway. The Norwegian government seized the opportunity to launch a major policy initiative to adapt the Norwegian economy to the challenge of world recession. Most notable was a counter-cyclical policy which held unemployment below 2% in a period which saw Scotland's unemployment rise to 8%. Institutional innovations included the creation of Statoil, a state-owned oil company, as the vehicle for the state's 'carried interest' in oil developments. Of equal significance was the close collaboration between the Norwegian government and Norwegian business in maximising Norway's industrial benefit from its natural wealth.

The prospect of oil wealth also extended the horizons of Norwegian policy-makers beyond economics. The first in the series of Norway's Long-Term Economic Programmes gave priority to making Norway a 'qualitatively better society' through a narrowing of income differentials, the decentralisation of power, sexual equality and a commitment to generous levels of aid to developing countries.

The wave of reforms which began in Quebec with the 'Quiet Revolution' of the 1960s perhaps owed less to economic causes than developments in Norway or Alberta. But the strengthening of Quebec's role as an exporter of hydro-electricity energy underpinned the rise of the nationalist Parti Quebecois in the 1970s. While the new party had some success in attracting the support of working-class Quebecers its cadres came from the rapidly expanding public-sector salariat recruited from an educational system which had been modernised and freed from the control of Catholic clerics in the 1960s. Quebec provides a clear example of the transformation of a traditionalist defensive nationalism into an aggressive reforming Nationalism.

The Scottish response to the discovery and revaluation of its oil assets was altogether more modest. The creation of the Scottish Development Agency in 1975 represented the only institutional development of note to put against Alberta's Energy Board and Heritage Trust, against Statoil or Hydro-Quebec. But by the end of the decade the amount of money made available for industrial investment by the Scottish Development Agency was far closer to the subsequent cuts in the annual value of other forms of regional assistance – approximately £70m – than to the £5bn which the oil revenues contributed to the London Exchequer in those years.

There remained the proposals for a Scottish Assembly as a token of Scotland's will be innovate. But whatever the historic and symbolic value of an Assembly, its powers would have been dwarfed by the scale of the opportunities opening up for Scotland. It would have had fewer powers than the Generalitat restored to Catalonia by the 1978 referendum, fewer than the German Lander, fewer even than the Greenland Parliament endorsed by the 23,000 voters of Greenland in January 1979. As a test of the will to innovate across-the-social-spectrum Assembly referendum showed the middle class as the least enthusiastic section of Scottish society, with only 35% of AB voters intending to vote 'Yes' in February 1979 compared with 65% of DE voters.[2]

Of course the response to the Assembly proposals provides only the crudest of measures. After all, the proposals provoked opposition even from committed Nationalists whose will for change can be taken as read. What continues to astonish fifteen years or so later is not so much the hostility or indifference of the majority of the Scottish middle class to the Assembly legislation but the weakness of their gut response to the dramatic change in Scotland's potential in the 1970s.

Why did Scotland's business community not seize the opportunity of Scotland's new wealth to secure a major adjustment of the economic balance in favour of Scotland, as the business class did in Alberta? Why did Scotland's public administrators not demand the opportunity to prove their capacity for 'nation-building' in the way the state bureaucracy of Quebec had been doing since the 1960s? Why were Scotland's 'caring' professions so loath to demand that Scotland's new wealth be applied to reducing the poverty and deprivation that blighted the lives of so many Scots, in the spirit of the Norwegian programme for welfare reform? Why did Scotland's health professionals not insist that they be given the means to launch new programmes of community health and health education among a population whose health record was abysmal by the standards of Western European countries? Why were Scottish architects and designers not clamouring for the public commissions which would challenge them to shape a new public face for Scotland in the way that Alvar Alto and his colleagues gave architectural expression to Finland's post-war revival? Why did Scotland's university teachers and administrators not seize the moment to demand major new provision for research to challenge the dominance of Oxford, Cambridge and London, and lay the basis for a bid to make Scotland once again an international centre of learning and inquiry? Why, in short, did the Scottish middle class in this moment of blossoming opportunity evince so little ambition for the public welfare of Scotland, or even for their own and their children's career prospects in Scotland?

Social and historical factors can be offered in speculative explanation. As noted earlier the core middle-class groups of employers, managers and professional workers formed a smaller proportion of the population in Scotland in 1971 than of the populations of England and Wales, 11.6% compared to 13.5%.[3] And the gap had widened slightly by 1981 with 13.4% of the Scottish population in these groups compared to 16.3% in England and Wales.[4] But this difference is too small to be taken seriously as an explanation.

Other structural factors concealed by an analysis based on occupational groups may have been at work. One such is the displacement of Scots by non-Scots in decision-taking posts in Scotland. The takeover of Scottish businesses by non-Scottish companies has been a matter of public debate in Scotland for decades. By the mid-seventies 40% of Scotland's manufacturing labour force worked in companies controlled from outwith Scotland along with a significant but unquantified proportion of Scotland's service industries. The record shows that takeover often led to a loss of top decision-taking jobs within the company and the loss of business for Scottish professional and other service companies as contracts were moved south. Where the top jobs remained in Scotland it became more likely that they would be filled by non-Scots.

Even where there has been no transfer of ownership or control a process of displacement of Scots by non-Scots in top jobs seems to have been taking place. Public-sector employers have increasingly recruited managerial and professional staff from a UK if not international labour market. The high proportion of non-Scots among the teaching staff of Scottish universities was actively debated in the early 1970s.[5] During the seventies non-Scots were becoming steadily more numerous in top jobs in other sectors: local government administration and services, the arts, the voluntary organisations. It is conceivable that this displacement hindered the growth of a 'critical mass' of Scottish concern and ambition.

Another factor which may have operated to obstruct the growth of a clear Scottish focus was the absence of independent trade union structures across a wide range of public-sector employment, in particular the fast-growing local government services. This has not always prevented public-sector employees in Scotland pursuing their distinct strategies in industrial disputes but it has certainly restricted the role of the trade unions as a base for independent Scottish initiative. The political initiatives of the Scottish Trades Union Congress provided partial compensation but in the 1970s the STUC was not active across such a wide range of Scottish issues of Scottish concern as it has been under the leadership of Campbell Christie in the 1980s.

These factors of displacement and assimilation were, of course, not operating in the traditional middle classes of the church, law and school teaching which recruited from a protected Scottish labour market. Surely these traditional professions with their key roles as carriers of Scottish identity would be eager to seize the moment for *'unde grade revanche'* for the centuries of subordination to English middle-class models and traditions rooted in London, Cambridge and Oxford?

But though they were still nationally distinct these groups were exposed to other factors which may have confined their political horizons. The Church of Scotland was clearly an institution in decline, both numerically and in social status. Although historically Scotland's national church, the Catholic Church was beginning to overhaul it in terms of members. Its General Assembly might still claim the title of 'Scotland's Parliament' but its deliberations were received by the public more and more as one voice among many, religious and secular, advertising their views on Scotland's future.

While the teaching profession had a firmer social base – its numbers had grown by 60% since the early 1950s – its members felt that their social and economic status was declining. The prolonged 'work-to-rule' actions of 1973-76 were symptoms of a deep unease about the profession's prospects and social role.

By comparison the Scottish legal profession seemed secure in its social status and economic prospects. But even here there were uncertainties. Scots Law was constantly exposed to the danger of erosion and injury by ignorant legislators. And in some of the fastest-growing and most lucrative areas of legal practice – tax law, administrative law, company law – the law was more British than Scottish and the opportunities were concentrated in London.

A further factor inhibiting the growth of radicalism among these traditional middle-class groups is their status as beneficiaries of the 'historic compromise' between English and Scottish interests built on the Act of Union of 1707. That settlement secured a position of provincial privilege within the emerging imperial state of Great Britain for the Church of Scotland, Scots Law and Scottish education. The privileges of Church and Law followed directly from the Act itself. The entrenchment of the privileges of the teaching profession was a longer process marked by the formation of the Scotch Education Department in 1874 and of the General Teaching Council for Scotland in 1966.

The benefits have been significant. The lawyers have enjoyed a protected market, the prestige of serving an imperial state and the prospect of promotion to senior legal office, not excluding the Lord Chancellorship of England. The Church of Scotland gained recognition as the National Church, and enjoyed the social privileges which went with that role. The teachers eventually gained a protected labour market, professional autonomy, membership of Scotland's educational 'policy community', and even – they could argue – preferential financial provision for Scottish education.

The 'historic compromise' thesis can be applied beyond these three historic middle-class interests. Scottish business benefited by trading its protected market for access to expanding markets in England and her colonies. In the twentieth century the growth of the Scottish Office provided a 'semi-protected' market in well-paid administrative jobs. The devolved structure of broadcasting in Scotland, with its 'semi-protected' market, can be seen as a late product of the compromise.

However, as an explanation of the conservatism of the Scottish middle classes the thesis is of limited value. The compromise provided the Church of Scotland with no protection against the Veto Act which led to the Disruption of 1843, Scots Law with no protection against the growth of law into new areas on an English foundation. It could never have provided protection against long-term secular trends such as the decline in Church membership, the loss of prestige by British state institutions, the impact of social and cultural changes on the attraction of teaching as a career. And of course it cannot apply to the wide range of middle-class professions which have never enjoyed any Scottish 'privilege'.

Scotland's main political parties have reinforced rather than challenged the conservatism of the Scottish middle class. They have at once reflected and institutionalised middle-class inhibitions.

In the 1970s the historic unionism of the Scottish Conservatives was reinforced by the hostility of Scotland's business community to any change in Scotland's political status. The base of this opposition lay in the West of Scotland industrial leadership represented by such figures as Lord Weir. It judged that even the modest change proposed in Labour government's devolution proposals would impose unacceptable costs on the business community, producing a left-wing socialist administration committed to the class war and to punitive taxation on business and leading to an independent Scotland cut off by tariff walls from its traditional markets in England and overseas.

This was a notable case of thinking with the blood rather than with the head. Such fears were a direct legacy of the Scottish engineering industry's history of bitter labour disputes and its traditional dependence on government war contracts and imperial markets. That they were still so salient in the 1970s owes much to the fact that the confidence Scottish manufacturing industry in general – and the West of Scotland engineering industry in particular – had been undermined by a crisis of closures and takeovers.

There were dissenting voices within the business community. Some of the 'Young Turks' of Edinburgh's financial community such as Ian Noble and Angus Grossart argued on cultural as well as economic grounds for a Scottish Assembly. It was significant that they were innovators in an economic sector which was expanding, had no history of labour militancy, had never been dependent on government contracts and was used to operating across national frontiers. But even in the financial sector theirs were minority voices. The big Scottish insurance companies and the clearing banks remained hostile or at best determinedly sceptical.

Indeed it was in the financial sector that the defensiveness and lack of confidence of the Scottish business community was most dramatically revealed when in 1981 the Scottish public learned that the Board of the Royal Bank of Scotland was seeking a takeover bid from the Standard Chartered Bank. Despite much expert opinion to the contrary, the directors of the Royal Bank maintained that the bank – which provided approximately one half of all Scotland's banking services – was too small to expand internationally by itself. Ironically the independence of the bank was finally secured by the London-based Monopolies and Mergers Commission. Denied its preferred option, the Royal Bank demonstrated that contrary to the wisdom of its own Board it did after all have the resources to diversify successfully within the UK and abroad.

Under such defeatist influence the Scottish Conservative Party showed no inclination to respond directly to the change in Scotland's external circumstances. It did respond to the internal challenge of the emergence of the Scottish National Party. From Edward Heath's Declaration of Perth in 1968 in support of the principle of a Scottish Assembly it had moved by 1974 to endorsing the call for a Scottish Oil Fund. But that marked the limit of official Conservatism's tolerance of nationalist aspirations. On assuming leadership of the party in 1975 Mrs Thatcher began hauling in the line. By the time of the 1979 referendum the Conservative Party was sharing the leadership of the 'No' campaign with its allies in the business community.

But by 1979 the Conservative Party shared its role as political representative of the middle class in Scotland. It retained a bare majority (53%) of the electoral support of the upper middle-class in the 1979 election but only 43% of the lower middle-class vote, the Labour, Liberal and Scottish National Parties attracted respectively 18, 15 and 14% of the upper middle-class vote and 30, 9 and 17% of the lower middle-class vote.[6]

By classic nationalist precedent the Scottish National Party should, at least, have been a keen rival to the Conservatives for the Scottish middle-class vote. But the SNP was a classic bourgeois party only in the sense that its leadership was drawn from the professional middle class of solicitors, teachers, doctors, journalists and accountants along with small businessmen. It never won majority support from any cohesive middle-class interest. Traditionally it drew it support more evenly from across the social spectrum than the other parties.[7] When it was at its peak in the mid-seventies its additional support came not primarily from the middle-class groups but from the skilled manual workers in the eighteen to thirty-five age group.

The group which always seemed the least likely to support the Nationalists was precisely the core bourgeoisie of the business class, fearful of losing traditional markets and state support. The only major business figure to come out in support of the SNP was the maverick Sir Hugh Fraser. For the rest the SNP had to content itself with the support of smaller businessmen whose markets were predominantly local, and a sprinkling of management consultants and financial specialists. If the Scottish owners of the companies servicing the oil developments sometimes looked enviously at the advantages conferred on their Norwegian-owned counterparts by the Norwegian government's protection policies, their dependence in the short term on Whitehall and in the longer term on the multi-national oil companies deterred them from drawing any radical political conclusions.

Following the restraints on public expenditure imposed by the Labour government in 1976 the Nationalists might have been expected to attract more support from Scotland's public-sector salariat. That it did not do so may be attributed partly to the presumed increase in the number of non-Scots in influential positions, partly to the lack of clarity in SNP's own ideological position, and partly to the influence of British trade unions and the Labour Party itself.

The Labour Party was indeed the SNP's chief rival for the support of Scotland's 'deviant' middle-class voters. In 1979 it attracted more than twice the number of middle-class votes that the SNP attracted.

Significantly its lead was greatest among the lower middle-class voters where the bulk of the public-sector salariat was located. While the Liberal Party was a close rival of Labour and the SNP among upper middle-class voters it fell badly behind in its appeal to lower middle-class voters. Not surprisingly the Liberal Party led both Labour and the SNP in middle-class support as a proportion of total support for the party. Indeed the class profile of support for Labour and the SNP was very similar, with the upper middle class contributing 3% more of SNP's support than of Labour support and the lower middle class contributing 1% more of Labour support than of SNP support. The Liberal profile was much closer to the Conservative profile with both attracting levels of support from working-class voters 29-30% lower than the SNP and Labour.[8]

The Conservative Party's failure to attract a higher proportion of Scotland's middle-class votes no doubt owes something to traditional tensions between English and Scottish 'establishments' which persisted after the 'historic compromise' of the Union. But Labour's relative success in attracting Scottish middle-class support probably owes more to a perception of Labour as the champion of state intervention to correct regional inequalities, particularly economic inequalities. Beginning with Tom Johnston, the Labour Party had established itself as the party of a 'managed economy' with strong regional development policies. The climax of this approach was reached with the creation of the Scottish Development Agency to provide planning, leadership and finance for the Scottish economy. In the October 1974 election the Labour Party had advertised its plans for the Agency under the immodest slogan *Powerhouse Scotland*. From its position of weakness the Scottish business community was able to join other sections of Scottish opinion in welcoming the Agency as a powerful support for Scotland's economic development.

During the 1970s the Labour Party itself became noticeably more middle-class. A new generation of activists, many of them with 'public sector' middle-class jobs, emerged to claim leadership of Labour's local government in Eastern Scotland, although in the West and in Central Region the working-class trade union leadership proved more resilient. At both the national level and the parliamentary level Scottish Labour presented an increasingly middle-class face to the world. By the mid-seventies two-thirds of Scots Labour MPs had a middle-class background or education: by 1988 only thirteen out of forty-nine Scottish Labour MPs had a working-class occupational background.

As a vehicle for ambitious, politically minded middle-class Scots the Labour Party served to divert energy and concern away from

Scottish priorities to British political exigencies. It provided a system of political rewards based in London in which Scotland featured as a proving ground and rear base. This regionalist perspective obscured the scale of the changes in Scotland's external circumstances during the 1970s.

Even when the Labour Party's role is added to the wider inhibitions to which Labour's middle-class career politicians were heir the sum of explanation remains obstinately less than its parts. Each of the factors specific to the Labour Party – its vested interest in a British system of power, its ideological hostility to any threat to working-class unity, its institutional conservatism – were exposed to and failed the judgement of time. Scotland's record under Westminster governments of both parties in the 1960s and 1970s declared its own verdict on the effectiveness of London rule while the oil discoveries gave dramatic credibility to the alternatives. The reality and potential of Scotland were opposed to each other more directly than at any previous moment in Scotland's modern history. Yet few Scots Labour MPs demonstrated any zeal for their own government's constitutional proposals, modest as they were. Of those who did – John Mackintosh, Jim Sillars, Harry Ewing, Alex Eadie, John Robertson, Denis Canavan – it may be significant that only one, John Mackintosh, was from an established middle-class background.

How was it that personalities such as John Smith, Donald Dewar, Robin Cook and Gordon Brown were so little excited by the opportunities which the 1970s opened up for Scotland? By class and culture they should have been highly sensitive to the changing status and opportunities of their national community and institutions. All four were from the marrow of the Scottish middle class. Their fathers' professions were respectively a primary head teacher, a doctor, a high school rector and a Church of Scotland minister. All were educated at Scottish schools and universities. They were well informed about Scotland's circumstances: Cook and Brown had a special knowledge of Scotland's social problems. As professional politicians they had no excuse for underestimating the problems of obtaining remedies from Westminster. Here surely were the elements to fire a passion to redress Scotland's wrongs. Who, indeed, was better equipped than they to lead an alliance of Scotland's frustrated middle class and its hard-pressed working class in a campaign to secure the benefits of Scotland's new-found wealth for the Scottish people? Instead these exemplars of middle-class Scotland responded, grudgingly, only when their electoral base came under direct threat from Nationalism. Only one, Gordon Brown, showed any notable enthusiasm for constitutional change and then rather less enthusiasm than another, Robin Cook, put into opposing his own Labour government's proposals for a Scottish Assembly. The two lawyers meanwhile conveyed the impression that the whole issue was an unfortunate diversion from the real world of politics in the corridors of Westminster. It seemed that there was little room in these well-educated heads for the notion that Scotland might be facing an historic opportunity to escape at last from the cruelly lingering legacy of the Industrial Revolution or to vindicate the ideals of Scottish democracy. In these middle-class deadlands of the imagination history happened in other places.

Perhaps it is the lack of vitality of the middle-class Scottish imagination which brings us closest to the heart of the mystery about the Scottish middle class. There is a striking dearth in the recent imaginative literature in Scotland of middle-class characters and experience. Scottish fiction and drama have been dominated for the last three decades by images of working-class Scotland. William McIlvanney, Gordon Williams, Alan Sharp, James Kelman, John Byrne, Bill Bryden, Hector MacMillan, Archie Hind, Peter MacDougall, Agnes Owens: the roll-call of working-class Scots writers is extensive and impressive. Middle-class writers, or at least writers who use middle-class characters in their Scottish context, are rare birds by comparison. Only two writers – Robin Jenkins and Elspeth Davie – have persisted with middle-class themes. Other names can be cited – James All Ford, Stuart Hood, James Kennaway, Allan Massie. But Ford's best-known novel, *The Brave White Flag* (1961), is set in the Second World War, and Hood's novels are set in pre-war or early post-war periods. James Kennaway certainly knew how to conjure up the demons of the Scottish soul but his particular constituency was the Anglo-Scottish upper middle class from which he himself came. Massie's closest engagement with the contemporary Scottish middle classes, *One Night in Winter* (1984), is one of his less successful novels, particularly in its treatment of characters who are not of Massie's own Anglo-Scottish background. Significantly the most widely read modern novel of the Scottish middle class, *The Prime of Miss Jean Brodie*, was a glorious one-off for its author Muriel Spark. Scottish drama post-Bridie is even less well endowed with characters from the Scottish middle class.

Recent Scottish autobiography has also been dominated by working-class experience. Jimmy Reid, Jimmy Boyle, Ralph Glasser, Ian Jack, Jim Sillars, Molly Weir are among those who have written of their working-class background and upbringing. Again middle-class examples can be cited – Billy Wolfe's political autobiography *Scotland Lives* (1973) stand out – but the working-class bias of the output is overwhelming. Assuming that the bias reflects the tastes of

Scottish readers many middle-class Scots must identify more strongly with images of working-class Scotland than with images of middle-class Scotland.

The working-class dominance of Scottish imaginative and inter-pretative literature, poetry apart, is the mirror image of the situation in England where middle-class character and context dominate and working-class experience is marginalised. There are signs of a revival of middle-class confidence and vitality in other areas of Scottish culture (among them historical and political writing and journalism) but if the urge, and capacity, to articulate one's experience through reconstructing it imaginatively in fiction and drama is taken as the test then the 'inarticulate Scot' is revealed as typically middle-class not working-class. It seems that the Scottish working class has developed a keener sense of identity from its long record of struggle against harsh odds than the Scottish middle class has learned from its complacent enjoyment of provincial privilege.

The 1980s presented a sharp challenge to the complacency and inertia of the Scottish middle class. The domestic reforms of Mrs Thatcher's administrations proved a stronger stimulus to the Scottish middle class to reassess its role than the changes in Scotland's external environment had proved in the previous decade. By the end of the eighties there was hardly a section of the Scottish middle class which remained untouched by the Thatcherite revolution.

The middle class was only affected at the margins by the dramatic rise in unemployment which took place in the first five years of Mrs Thatcher's rule. It felt the impact of the Thatcherite economic whirlwind rather more through the accelerated destruction by closure or takeover, or both, of a very large part of what remained of a Scottish-controlled economic base. The list of victims included Distillers, Coats, Anderson Strathclyde, Stenhouse, Arthur Bell, Scottish Agricultural Industries, and United Wire. By 1986 half of the 140 biggest Scottish registered companies in 1979 were under external control.[9] While some Scots businessmen and commentators had armed themselves ideologically to accept the process as a necessary and invigorating part of the working of the market many others voiced their fears that the takeovers were part of a vicious circle of relative economic decline.

The public-sector middle class in Scotland was certainly not less exposed to the effects of Thatcherism. The Conservative cuts in public expenditure were targeted in particular at public services. With a smaller proportion of middle-class Scots than of middle-class English people opting out of the public health and education systems the Scottish middle class was more sensitive to the effect of government policy on the standard of the services. And with a higher proportion of the Scottish labour force dependent on the public sector for jobs – 34% compared to 30% in England – the Scottish middle class had greater reason to feel concerned about job security and career prospects.

Other government measures reinforced concerns about jobs and careers. The privatisation of state industries and public utilities reduced the government's political stake in the maintenance of the jobs and opened the way to market-led rationalisation. The push for privatisation of services provided by local authorities and health boards forced many middle-class employees to consider the options of returning to the private sector perhaps through management buy-outs. While primary and secondary education escaped significant job losses, higher and further education and state-financed research institutes lost jobs and security of tenure.

The Thatcherite campaign to recreate an enterprise society had a particular urgency in Scotland. Thatcherism diagnosed Scotland as an extreme example of the 'dependency culture' which had sapped the vitality of British society as a whole. In Scotland the disease of dependency had spread further through the social body than in England, disabling sections of both the working class and the middle class which should have been natural supporters of Mrs Thatcher's mission. Symptoms of the Scottish disease were found not only in Scotland's inability to generate the economic dynamism of the south of England but also in the electoral unpopularity of the Conservative Party under Mrs Thatcher's leadership. By the 1987 election the Conservative share of the two-party vote in the average Scottish constituency was nearly 20% below what it would have been if Scotland had voted in line with Britain as a whole,[10] and the proportion of the professional, administrative and managerial class voting for the Conservative Party fell below 30% in Scotland.[11]

Even before the debacle of 1987 the Conservative Party had been persuaded of the need for exceptional measures to stem the loss of middle-class support in Scotland. It responded to the dismay spread among the middle class in Scotland by domestic property revaluation of 1984 by pledging to replace the rates by a flat-rate community charge designed to relieve the middle class of its 'disproportionate' contribution to local government expenditure.

But the 1985 commitment to the poll-tax was a defensive measure. If the Conservative Party was to be revived in Scotland the Scottish middle class had to be persuaded to become active in Scottish public life in support of the ideal of a free market enterprise society.

The Thatcherite strategy for a middle-class revival in Scotland had two elements. It sought first to create new opportunities and incentives for the Scottish middle class to assume a leadership role in Scottish society. And it contrived, secondly, to polarise Scottish opinion between a public sector, corporatist interest on the one hand and a private-sector free-market interest on the other.

Public authorities had already been put under severe expenditure constraints by the government. Local authorities were now to be subjected to the further political constraint created by the replacement of the roughly progressive property tax by a regressive poll-tax. Having bound the public-sector victim the government then invited the middle class led by the business sector to despoil his assets.

Councils were legally required to put designated services out to competitive tender while the government actively promoted the 'contracting out' of a wider range of local authority and health services. Health Boards were shamelessly packed with Conservative supporters or Thatcherite fellow-travellers. The power of the health professions was curbed by new styles of business management and new forms of funding and by government encouragement to hospital management to initiate 'opting-out'. College Councils were placed under business leadership and given new management powers. Universities were forced to move closer to the market by cuts in public funding. The creation of School Boards presented middle-class parents with the opportunity through the 'opting-out' option to transfer even more of their social privileges to their offspring, largely at public expense.

The climax of these government efforts to recreate a private-sector middle-class leadership came with the proposal to merge the training functions of the Training Agency in Scotland with the economic development role of the Scottish Development Agency in a new body called Scottish Enterprise. Both the Central Board and the Boards of the twenty-two Local Enterprise Companies which Scottish Enterprise will fund to deliver training and economic development services locally are to have a statutory two-thirds majority of businessmen.

The advance claims made for the economic effectiveness of Scottish Enterprise rest on highly contentious ideological assumptions about the sources of wealth creation. What is clear is that with an annual budget of £500m Scottish Enterprise represents – in intention – a massive transfer of power from the public to the private sector. For a Government ideologically opposed to state intervention it is an audacious piece of social engineering.

In response to the impact of Thatcherism the 1980s have seen a wider range of middle-class interventions in Scottish politics than in any other post-war decade.

Provoked by the introduction of School Boards the Educational Institute of Scotland abandoned its preference for 'insider' lobbying to appeal directly to Scottish opinion in a campaign against the Anglicisation of Scotland's educational system. Scottish doctors and consultants canvassed public support for their opposition to government plans to extend the role of market forces in the health services. The Association of University Teachers reversed its former opposition to the universities' inclusion in the responsibilities of the Scottish Assembly to campaign for their inclusion in future schemes for a Scottish Parliament, a position now endorsed by the Principals of the Scottish universities. The Church of Scotland and the Catholic Church have been forthright in their condemnation not just of specific Thatcherite policies but of the whole Thatcherite ethos. The Standing Commission on the Scottish Economy under the chairmanship of a former Principal of a Scottish university detailed a 'democratic corporatist' alternative to Thatcherism for the Scottish economy.[12] Scotland's two 'quality' daily newspapers, *The Scotsman* and the *Glasgow Herald*, along with *Scotland on Sunday* and *Observer Sunday*, have been unremittingly critical of the application of Thatcherism in Scotland. Both the Faculty of Advocates and the Law Society of Scotland have publicised their case against the government's proposed legal reforms. While the focus of the campaign for the non-payment of the poll-tax has been on the Anti-Poll Tax Unions with their militant leadership and largely working-class constituency, the ranks of non-payers embrace many tens of thousands of principled middle-class non-payers.

The most significant evidence of a radicalisation of Scottish middle-class attitudes is found in the publication of *A Claim of Right for Scotland* by the Scottish Constitutional Convention asserting the sovereign right of the Scottish people to determine its own constitutional future.[13] Although the Convention was set up by a broad coalition of Scotland's oppositional groups – the churches, trade unions, local authorities, political parties – the committee which drafted the Claim was conspicuously 'bourgeois', embracing a former chief planner at the Scottish office, a former member of the British Diplomatic Service, a regius professor of Public Law, a former convener of the Church and Nation Committee of the Church of Scotland, the chairman of the Scottish Postal Board, and a former under-secretary at the Scottish Office. As well as being an expression of a more radical mood the Convention exerted its own radicalising influence on the debate about Scotland's constitutional options. It stimulated new thinking about the voting system, and about the need for regional balance in a Scottish Parliament. It also provided a moral support and a source of leverage for Scottish Labour Action, a grouping of Labour MPs and activists who wanted to push the Labour Party towards a more radical form of devolution embracing proportional representation and backed by a doctrine of a 'dual' Scottish and British mandate.

The most noteworthy evidence of a mobilisation of middle-class opinion on the political Right was the formation in May 1989 of the Scottish Business Group (SBG) to promote more active support by businessmen at local level for the Conservative Party. The group included some big names such as James Gulliver, Sir Hector Laing and Sir Ian MacGregor whose business interests were not primarily Scottish, along with a wide cross-section of the leaders of Scottish business. According to reports it was at meetings of the core group of the SBG that the proposals for Scottish Enterprise were developed. The Group also played a key part in persuading the Scottish Office to back down on its opposition to unifying business rates on both sides of the border.[14] A key figure in the SBG was Bill Hughes who launched the idea for Scottish Enterprise while chairman of the Confederation of British Industry in Scotland and who later became vice-chairman of the Scottish Conservative Party. A symptom of the polarisation of Scottish opinion which the Thatcher years had produced was the presence in the core group of the financier Angus Grossart who in the 1970s had been an advocate of a Scottish Assembly. Bill Hughes was closely associated with the restructuring of the Scottish Conservative Party carried out by the new chairman Michael Forsyth with the aim of bringing in younger, ideologically more militant organisers to pep up Conservative campaigning in the constituencies.

There were only a few other signs of a mobilisation of the Scottish middle class in the Thatcherite cause. The Adam Smith Institute publicised a free-market agenda for Scottish politics, although unfortunately for its political credibility the poll-tax was its best known contribution to government policy. The *Sunday Times Scotland* supplement provided a platform for free-market, or at least conservative opinion, most notably through the contributions of novelist Allan Massie. A group of Conservative if not Thatcherite ministers and elders was reported in 1989 to be organising within the Church of Scotland to challenge the dominance of the anti-Thatcherites. And there were isolated instances of groups of doctors and hospital managers with government encouragement braving the disapproval of colleagues, unions, Health Councils and local politicians by floating proposals for local hospital 'opt-outs'.

The evidence of middle-class mobilisation to support or oppose Thatcherism is clear enough. But it adds up to something less than a revolution in the public aspirations of the Scottish middle class.

There are few signs that the poll-tax is beginning to persuade a wider section of Scottish opinion that the local state needs to be drastically pruned back. Nor is there any evidence to date that a significant number of Scottish parents are likely to take advantage of the 'opting-out' provision in the Conservatives' education reforms. It seems that Scottish opinion has been unimpressed by the government's attempts at social engineering on the educational front.

Equally very few doctors and consultants have shown any inclination to follow government exhortations and incentives to take advantage of the new market opportunities in the health field. What little there has been in the way of positive response has been initiated by hospital managers acting with ideologically committed Health Boards or by straightforward commercial interests. Although the 'force majeure' of legislation and government economic coercion is affecting a significant change in the balance between private and public sectors in Scotland the Scottish middle class seems disinclined to discard its collectivist habits in favour of Thatcherite individualism.[15]

Apostles of the market may find more reason to be optimistic about the chances of creating a new generation of business leadership. Certainly Scottish Enterprise has attracted significant support from the business community at both national and local levels. But Scottish Enterprise still has everything to prove. Many of the businessmen who have declared their support for the Local Enterprise Companies would probably not subscribe to the claims Bill Hughes made for the inherent superiority of businessmen over public authorities in economic development and training. Some leading businessmen have expressed doubts about the compatibility of market-led entrepreneurship and public accountability. Others fear that effective power will in any case rest with the public servants transferred from the Training Agency and the Scottish Development Agency and with central government.

In any case the private-sector base on which a new business leadership must be built is very weak. As we have seen external takeover has reduced Scottish ownership in manufacturing to a minority interest. Scotland has one of the worst records of new firm formation of any region.[16] It is difficult to accept at face value claims for a glorious revival of Scottish business confidence when a spokesman such as Professor Jack Shaw of Scottish Financial Enterprise, representing the most dynamic sector of the Scottish economy, insists that legislative devolution would cripple the Scottish economy, as if political decentralisation had crippled the bankers of Basel and Zurich, Boston and Houston, Frankfurt and Hamburg, Barcelona and Madrid.

There remains an unresolved dilemma at the heart of the free-market evangelism of the Scottish Business Group. Is the full rigour of the market to be applied to Scotland even if that means the final elimination of Scotland's business autonomy in an integrating world? The Adam Smith Institute would argue that the elimination of Scottish ownership and control from the 'mature' sectors of the economy would simply be the prelude to a rebirth of Scottish enterprise on a more competitive and sustainable basis in new sectors. Whether such faith could withstand the rest of a takeover of the Royal Bank of Scotland, Standard Life, Scottish and Newcastle or the Wood Group is doubtful. After the debacle of the Trustee Savings Bank, the loss of Distillers, the failure to secure any clear corporate advantage for Scotland from the sale of Britoil and British Gas, the pressure for political intervention would be intense. It is worth asking whether any significant section of the Scottish business class will maintain its ideological zeal for the market beyond the term of Mrs Thatcher's premiership. With Mrs Thatcher gone, Michael Forsyth and Bill Hughes lose their political base, even their political *raison d'être*. Freed from the bullying of the Scottish Office and Conservative Party headquarters it is not improbable that many businessmen would want to restore, if not old-style Scottish corporatism at least the sort of collaborative relations with the public sector typical of other European economies.

If the prospect of Scotland being transformed into an 'enterprise' society in the Thatcherite image is remote, there are question marks too over the political significance and staying power of the 'oppositional' middle-class activism of the last five years. The only theme obviously common to all the opposition campaigns, from teachers to lawyers, is resistance to the application of market prescriptions to their respective occupational sectors or professional concerns. Constitutional reform does not qualify as a unifying theme. The representative organisation for some of the oppositional groups – school and university teachers, the Churches – have declared their support for one form or other of legislative devolution for Scotland. But the professional organisations of the socially more powerful doctors and lawyers have not – and probably will not – take a stance on the issue however clear their interest in the creation of a Scottish legislature may appear to observers.

The oppositional campaigns are perhaps best understood as part of a syndrome of Scottish resistance to Thatcherism which draws its strength from a combination of mutually supporting factors. One is Scotland's greater dependence on the public sector. Another is the common perception that the liberalisation of markets will handicap rather than benefit Scotland. Another is the widespread belief that Mrs Thatcher was instinctively unsympathetic to Scotland, symbolised for many by her categoric rejection of the case for a Scottish legislature. Yet another is the higher level of commitment by Scottish opinion to such core social democratic values as a preference for welfare spending over tax cuts, for public rather than private provision of social services, of a belief in collective rather than individual responsibility for unemployment.

None of these factors is immune from change. Mrs Thatcher has gone. As privatisation is extended Scotland's dependence on the public sector will diminish. Social democracy is on the defensive if not in retreat in most parts of Europe. If Scotland remains loyal does that represent a source of radical energy, or is it due to a time-lag between developments in Scotland and developments elsewhere? What is clear is that if the oppositional middle-class groups do represent a potential source of radical energy, an effective catalyst for their political development and coalescence is still wanting.

The opinion polls in the spring of 1990 suggested that the Labour Party may have been the chief electoral beneficiary in Scotland of middle-class opposition to Thatcherism. But the Labour Party has its own interests to pursue. Whatever the electoral auguries, it is still ideologically on the retreat from Thatcherism and preoccupied with adapting its policies to the interests and values of the voters in the Midlands and South of England. It is more interested in containing than in catalysing Scottish disaffection. By early 1989 the party had declared against a campaign of non-payment of the poll-tax, thus surrendering the opportunity simultaneously of defending the weakest members of Scottish society, inflicting a major defeat on Thatcherism and vindicating Scotland's political claims. By the end of the year Robin Cook, the only senior party spokesman to declare himself a non-payer, was insisting that his stance was purely a personal one and that he would not be urging it on the party, an apt illustration of the Labour Party's disabling effect on Scotland's civic conscience. By early 1990 the Labour Party's Scottish leadership had succeeded in containing the advance of the more radical spirits grouped in Scottish Labour Action. It had won conference approval to reinterpret the *Claim of Right* as little more than a statement of the right of the Scottish people to vote in Westminster elections. It had secured the rejection of the 'dual mandate' reserving the right of the Scottish people to determine their own future in the event of Scotland again voting for Labour while England returned another Conservative majority. The drive for a clear commitment to proportional representation had been diverted into a party study of alternative electoral systems. Thus the Scottish Labour leadership had secured its political base in preparation for another bid for the ultimate, deceiving, prize of sovereign power at Westminster.

Meanwhile the Scottish National Party had weakened its credentials as a catalysing force by its ill-judged withdrawal from the Scottish Constitutional Convention. Not that the SNP had shown much inclination to extend its campaigning fronts to respond to the spread of middle-class disaffection. In 1989, despite Jim Sillars's 1988 Govan by-election promise that SNP would promote a broad anti-Thatcher coalition, the party opted for a strategy of polarising anti-Thatcherite opinion on two different axes: payment or non-payment of the poll-tax and support or opposition to Scotland's independent membership of the European Community. In these confrontations other issues such as the future of the Health Service, poverty, the environmental crisis, the future of Scottish education, were sidelined. The SNP had lost its capacity to seize the policy initiative except over a very narrow range of issues. Like the Labour Party it failed conspicuously to articulate an alternative to the Thatcherite vision of the 'enterprise' society. Indeed its uncritical enthusiasm for embrace of the European Community's single internal market suggested an indifference to the effect of closer European integration on the more vulnerable members of Scottish society.

With its radical prospectus and middle-class identity the Scottish Constitutional Convention appeared in its earlier days in 1988 to have potential as a catalysing force for middle-class disaffection. But the Convention has been revealed as too much a creature of vested political interests: the Labour Party, the Scottish Trades Union Congress (STUC), the Convention of Scottish Local Authorities (COSLA), the churches. To retain political credibility it has had to conform to the electoral strategy and timetable of the Labour Party. Weakened by the SNP withdrawal it has failed to establish its own political identity. By the end of 1989 it appeared more as a forum for bargaining between political interests – notably the Labour Party and the Liberal Democrats but also the radical elements within the Labour Party – than an independent source of political ideas and action. Crucially, by failing to proclaim its definition of Scotland's right as the moral basis of the poll-tax non-payment campaign it surrendered the opportunity to vindicate the constitutional radicalism of the *Claim of Right* by applying it to the political issue of the moment. The Convention's failure was emblematic of the failure of any prominent middle-class Scots outwith a sprinkling of MPs and Nationalist leaders publicly to proclaim the doctrine of justified defiance of the poll-tax legislation.

Scottish developments cannot be judged by events in Eastern or Baltic Europe. But the comparison helps to highlight a major defect in the structure of political dissent in Scotland. In the Eastern

European countries the Communist monopoly of power forced the opposition to create new, informal structures of civic and intellectual dissent which owed no loyalty to the establishment. In Scotland, as the record of the Convention illustrates, political opposition is heavily institutionalised in organisations such as the Labour Party, the STUC and COSLA which have a powerful vested interest in controlling and limiting the growth of dissent. Even if there had been a more powerful moral and intellectual impulse in Scotland towards a radical critique of the political system, these vested interests would have moved quickly to block the formation of independent centres of organisation.

Even so there are some grounds for believing that the Scottish middle class will adopt a more radical political stance in the 1990s. First the events of the 1980s have loosened the social and economic moorings of key sections of the middle class including university teachers, school teachers, doctors and public sector managers and administrators. It seems unlikely that a change of government within the United Kingdom will restore the old 'corporatist' order in Scotland. Important elements of Thatcherism – a belief in consumer rights, a new balance between public and private provision, enhanced concern for 'value for money', greater scope for the contracting out of public services, the liberalisation of the market in professional services – will survive the passing of Thatcherism and reinforce the social impact of longer-term changes in the economic structure.

Second, the infrastructure of middle-class debate outwith the vested political interests has been strengthened. Although the Scottish universities have failed to contribute proportionately to their intellectual resources to the reassessment of Scottish needs and opportunities, their experience in the 1980s has made them more committed to Scotland both politically and intellectually. The Scottish media have diversified and strengthened their contribution with the growth of the Scottish quality press and a more confident presentation of Scottish issues on television. There is now a significant grouping of Scottish 'think-tanks' with varying degrees of independence from political sponsors, from the Nationalist Centre for Social and Economic Research and the Labour John Wheatley Centre at one end of the spectrum to Edinburgh University's Centre for Theology and Public Issues, the Red-Green conferences and the Free University of Glasgow at the other end.

Environmental issues are bound to impinge more and more forcefully on political debate, forcing a reassessment of the conventional political and economic priorities. The infant Scottish Green Party is already exerting an influence on Scottish debate out of all proportion to its numbers. It is the only party which shows any appreciation of the challenge which European integration presents to the ideal of participatory democracy.

The European factor will also have an increasing impact on the Scottish debate. In the shape of the European Community's single internal market it will expose sections of the middle class including Scottish businessmen and professional groups to increased competition. Its free-market bias will create a further obstacle to the restoration of the old 'corporatist' order in Scotland.

European integration within and without the frontiers of the European Community will also increase the economic pressures for a more direct and coherent Scottish response. At one level it will generate support for a direct Scottish voice in the management of European integration on the same basis as other comparably sized member nations. At another, as the discretionary powers of national governments are restricted by the process of integration it will increase pressure for the politically co-ordinated Scottish response in the still unrestricted policy areas to minimise Scotland's disadvantages and maximise her opportunities in the new single market.

But perhaps the most important effect of European integration will be to accelerate the erosion of the 'dual' Scottish-British identity which in the 1970s John P. Mackintosh was championing as a constraint on the growth of Scottish Nationalism.[17] Mackintosh's argument was a valuable reminder in the heat of the Nationalist debate of the 1970s that most Scots, particularly middle-class Scots, saw themselves as both British and Scottish. But Mackintosh's argument gives insufficient weight to the fact that national identity is a dynamic not a static quantity and that discounts the duty of intellectuals constantly to assess and redefine myths of national identity against the changing needs and opportunities of their national community.

The advance of European integration makes that task more urgent. Integration both increases the incentive to change and secures the opportunity for change without the perceived risks of 'separation'. That may well prove to be the formula which breaks down at least the outer defences of Scottish middle-class conservatism. The growth of positive will to radical action on Scotland's behalf may depend on a more profound Europeanisation of the Scottish imagination in which the Scottish middle class learns to see itself equally with the Scottish working class as the hero and heroine of its own nation's history.

9

Conclusion

Mrs Thatcher's resignation from the premiership occurred at the time that most of the contributions to this volume had come in and a general election will have been held either shortly before or (the likelier prospect) within twelve months of this book appearing in print.

Scots were largely spectators watching from afar the internal power struggle which laid low Mrs Thatcher. Admittedly, the engine of her destruction, the poll-tax, had been summoned into life by the energetic lobbying of Thatcher loyalists in Scotland galvanised by the threat to the Tory electoral base posed by a looming re-evaluation of property in the mid-1980s. By the time of her departure, the élan of these ultras had already been dented by the eclipse of her apostle in Scotland, Michael Forsyth (although he still clung to ministerial office).

The credibility of long-distance-rule from London has suffered enormously, both from the poll-tax fiasco and the junking of sacred principles concerning fiscal responsibility by Michael Heseltine, the Environment Minister, in an attempt to get rid of 'the body' before a general election. Indeed an issue as apparently innocuous as local government finance has revealed the expediency and short-term outlook that has regulated the affairs of government even under a ruler like Margaret Thatcher, imbued with a philosophy and a plan for government. The huge amounts of money, running into millions, used to administer, shore up, and then bury the poll-tax monster are an indictment of blind centralist control. It will be exceedingly difficult in the future for Tory Unionists to present themselves as champions of inexpensive government whose quarrel with a self-governing assembly for Scotland is that it would simply be a costly additional tier of government.

In April 1991 an opinion poll carried out among Tory supporters in Scotland by *The Sunday Times* revealed an altered political landscape. 60% of Tories expressed support for a form of separate assembly, 34% of them (the majority) favouring the Scottish Constitutional Convention's proposal for an assembly with the power to make laws and levy taxes.[1] This apparent re-think on the part of a largely middle-class sector of the electorate may not be the only consequence flowing from the weakened legitimacy of a government which traded on the fact that unitary Westminster government stood for continuity and competence, but it is certainly one of the most startling. Signs of middle-class restlessness even in the unionist *laager* bear out – albeit in a surprising way – Stephen Maxwell's contention that the 1990s were likely to see further signs of middle-class radicalisation in Scotland.

However, unionist disarray has not rebounded to the benefit of the most radical exponents of self-government, the SNP. The Mori poll carried in *The Sunday Times* on 28 April 1991 put its electoral support at 15% with Alex Salmond's popularity falling to its lowest level since he assumed the party leadership in 1990. Along with other senior office-bearers, he continues to adhere to a brand of conviction politics which once had been the trademark of Margaret Thatcher and in its adversarial approach could be summed up as 'bash the opposition at every turn'. The tenor of a speech made to the party faithful by Salmond in March 1991 reveals no self-doubt about a form of partisanship which proved so counter-productive for Thatcher and Scottish acolytes such as Michael Forsyth:

> The other parties are devoid of principle and vision. The Tories are in headlong retreat as they ditch Thatcher's policies. Labour, having moved on to the Thatcherite agenda to chase the yuppie vote in the south of England, is now left high and dry. As for the Democrats, they will do deals with anyone.[2]

Such combativeness is perhaps excusable in the context of a looming election but it has been the stock-in-trade of the SNP whatever the political season. Undoubtedly the vehemence of the party towards its opponents gives it a higher profile but there is no sign that it has proved electorally rewarding: despite 80%+ support for self-government, the party's support remains at a level which would make it difficult to retain all of its five seats or pick up new ones.

One of these seats belongs to Dick Douglas, a Labour MP who defected to the SNP in 1990. At a special conference in March 1991 party rules were changed to enable him to stand as a SNP candidate (he will be opposing Donald Dewar in Glasgow Garscadden) even though he has been a party member for less than the statutory minimum period. The future of the anti-poll-tax campaign was also on the agenda. This led to a bruising debate between a leadership in favour of winding up the campaign and rank-and-file activists who thought that there was still everything to fight for despite government plans to scrap the tax. In the end the leadership prevailed but the vote – 244 in favour 132 against – indicated the level of dissension.

The non-payment campaign was shelved and replaced with one entitled 'Protect the Poor' that was intended to defend those who would be on the receiving end of crippling poll-tax bills for years ahead. Jim Sillars broke ranks with erstwhile allies Kenny McAskill and Ian Lawson by coming down on the pragmatic side: 'how are we going to build the confidence of the Scottish people if, when they have won the best civil disobedience campaign in their history, we tell them they haven't done it'.[3]

But while the leadership repudiated a maximalist campaign on the poll-tax, fundamentalism was the order of the day in relation to the Scottish Constitutional Convention which according to Salmond stood for 'dependency in the United Kingdom'. The argument that the SNP had won a famous long-term victory by pushing self-government to the forefront of the agenda surely carried much more weight than the hyperbole associated with its anti-poll-tax campaign, but it was one that only a gradualist minority within the party seemed to grasp. Party spokespersons continued to pour scorn on a self-government scheme which continued to enjoy the backing of a clear majority of the electorate. Jim Sillars insisted early in 1991 that 'the only future for Scotland is to be a full partner state in the new Europe'.[4] In an alteration to the party's 'Independence in Europe' strategy he advocated a confederal Europe in which all the important powers within the European Community would be exercised by national governments acting in combination. This formula was preferable to 'a centralised federal Europe' in which such powers were exercised by a supra-national European government. According to constitutional expert Bob McCreadie, Sillars' vision of 'Independence in a Confederal Europe' is one shared by English nationalists like Margaret Thatcher and her supporters in the Bruges group.[5] However, the adjustments to the SNP's European policy were approved at a special March conference without any serious ructions, a small band of dissenters having earlier left to form a breakaway Scottish Sovereignty Movement.

Afterwards Alex Salmond briefly made headlines by floating the idea that Edinburgh would be an appropriate headquarters for the proposed European Central Bank. It was a smart initiative but it had the ring of dependency about it: Scotland would benefit as a result of a decision taken in a faraway power-centre with there being little local input into the arrangement.

The SNP has been devoid of ideas about how Scotland could play a role in the ferment which is transforming the shape of Europe from the Atlantic coast to the Urals. Other than a visit that Margaret Ewing paid to the Baltic States early in 1991, the SNP has not done anything substantial to support the efforts of three nations to recover their statehood. The Balts and at least some of the Scots have much in common by virtue of being nations who see their future being secured by full sovereign independence rather than by a pan-European regionalist solution which is the preferred option of stateless nations in western Europe. It is not difficult to imagine ways in which solidarity with the Baltic nations might have been advanced through insisting upon a parliamentary debate or making active representations to the Soviet embassy in London, or even going to Moscow and staging a protest in Red Square.

There are other ways in which the SNP might have strengthened its European profile. Given the unwillingness of the British government to promote the study of English and to promote cultural links with the emerging democratic nations of eastern Europe, the SNP might have glimpsed an opening here to solidify Scottish links with countries that could benefit from the intellectual resources to be found in a small country with eight universities and many other educational institutions.

Calls for a Scottish-funded English-language university based in eastern Europe or for regular exchanges that would enable young people to gain skills by training and working in Scottish institutions would have dented the party's image for insularity. This is the type of activity that would also fall within the remit of a future Scottish Assembly but the SNP is so absorbed with the electoral game that it is not surprising that it fails to grasp such initiatives that would increase Scotland's European profile and would involve it in offering its expertise rather than being the recipient of support offered from elsewhere. Scots-led schemes to help nations with far less going for them than this one would help to break down the passive mentality which suggests that Scotland is a place where things are done to people but where people have little opportunity to shape their own destiny or come to the aid of others.

In the first few months of 1991 there was no sense of expectation that stirring times might lie ahead for Scotland following a general election. Instead the palace revolution which removed Thatcher induced a perceptible feeling of anti-climax. Her successor, John Major, has lowered the political temperature but, on a visit to Scotland in January 1991, his description of the Constitutional Convention as 'a fraud, a joke, a Labour Party front which has decided nothing' suggested that he had either been reading Alex

Salmond's speeches or, more likely, that his provincial south-London outlook on the world has left him with an uncomprehending Thatcherite mind – set on constitutional issues.[6]

The sharp fluctuations in opinion poll ratings suggests that a close result is likely with no party enjoying an overall majority. The SNP is scarcely likely to hold the balance of power but it might enjoy considerable leverage along with the Liberal Democrats in the event of a hung parliament. It will be a test of SNP maturity if it can break out of its splendid isolation and co-operate across party barriers in such a crucial situation. A hopeful sign is Alex Salmond's admission that he would vote for a Scottish Parliament if the alternative choice was the constitutional status quo.[7] The Constitutional Convention already exists as a mechanism for such co-operation. If the SNP had taken part in its deliberations in the 1989-91 period, its poll rating would likely be considerably higher than the 15% at which it stood at the close of April 1991 and the party would have gone a long way to shake off its image of being a permanent oppositional force.

In the 1990s there is now in Scotland a greater understanding of the case for self-government, a greater self-confidence, a broader consensus and a more impressive line-up of leading figures to press the case. But disunity over goals and the means to achieve them could still produce a repeat of the 1979 fiasco which would remove from the agenda for the foreseeable future every plan for meaningful self-government, including the SNP's flagship of 'Independence in Europe'. The demise of *Radical Scotland* (having reached its fiftieth issue and with a circulation of under 4,000) which argued the case for a distinctive self-governing Scotland with more clarity and depth than any other journal (and from which the quote at the beginning of the paragraph is taken) shows how skin-deep the politicisation of the Scottish community is in many respects. It is doubtful if any SNP publication will fill the vacuum left by the gaping void in Scottish political journalism.

Parties as well as periodicals can wither and die, even in a context favourable to their aims, if they fail to connect with the popular mood. If the SNP continues to brand as opponents all those who fail to accept its goal of full sovereign independence it is in danger of cutting off its own life-support system and sliding into a twilight existence where it is kept alive by protest votes and illusory by-election 'breakthroughs'. Other Scottish parties have been gripped by the messianic self-righteousness which currently informs the actions and statements of the SNP. To find out about them it is necessary to consult the history books because they disappeared into obscurity having been an outlet for people's grievances but having failed to be a vehicle for their aspirations which is the secret of success in politics.

Whether the party can acquire the self-awareness and composure to grasp that its preferred strategy is only one among several routes towards Scottish emancipation, will determine its fate in a decade in which the Scottish electorate will probably be inclined to live dangerously and shelve its traditional pessimism, but only provided those committed to meaningful self-government in each party can abandon their mutual rivalry in British parliamentary elections and start building solid alliances. The SNP has more to gain from such an exercise than any other party. As long as it resists a strategy – one that would be grasped elsewhere in the small west European democracies like Norway or Denmark – it is endangering its future – and much else besides – out of a fixation with ideological purity.

10

References

Introduction

1. *Sunday Times*, 23 September 1990.

The SNP Faces the 1990s

1. M. Fry, *Patronage and Principle*, Aberdeen University Press, Aberdeen 1987, p 221.
2. *The Scotsman*, 29 July 1981.
3. J. Sillars, *Scotland, The Case for Optimism*, Polygon, Edinburgh 1986, pp 105, 110.
4. At the time of writing, the most comprehensive account of how the SNP and Labour reacted to the Convention is provided by I. McWhirter's article, 'After Doomsday . . . The Convention and Scotland's Constitutional Crisis', in *Scottish Government Yearbook, 1990*, Edinburgh University Press, Edinburgh 1990.
5. See J. Geekie and R. Levy, 'Devolution and the tartanisation of the Labour Party', *Parliamentary Affairs*, 42, 3, 1989.
6. *Scotland on Sunday*, 5 November 1989.
7. Letter from Ian O. Bayne, 31 January 1990.
8. *Sunday Times*, 13 November 1989.
9. *Marxism Today*, June 1988.
10. *New Statesman and Society*, 27 August 1990.
11. C. Harvie, *Scotland and Nationalism*, Allan & Unwin, London 1977, p 232.
12. *The Scotsman*, 29 August 1984.
13. A. McArthur and H. Kingsley Long, *No Mean City*, 1935.

Nationalism, Journalism and Cultural Politics

1. *The Times*, 31 August 1990.
2. See Neal Ascherson, 'Devolution Diary', in *Cencrastus*, No. 22, 1986, p 5; and Stephen Maxwell, 'The Nationalism of Hugh MacDiarmid', in

P. H. Scott, A. C. David (eds), *The Age of MacDiarmid: Essays on Hugh MacDiarmid and his Influence on Contemporary Scotland*, Mainstream, Edinburgh 1980, p 221.

3. J. Brand, *The National Movement in Scotland*, Routledge, London 1978, p 90.
4. Ibid., p 103.
5. Quoted by Angus Calder in 'Culture and Politics' in C. Harvie (ed), 'Towards a New Scotland', in *Cencrastus*, 1990.
6. Gallup Poll, *News Chronicle*, 16 January 1945; W. Miller, *The End of British Politics: Scots and English Political Behaviour in the Seventies*, OUP, Oxford, p 99; *Glasgow Herald*, 15 September 1988.
7. H. J. Hanham, *Scottish Nationalism*, Faber, London 1969, pp 146-162.
8. Ibid., p 175.
9. G. E. Davie, *The Democratic Intellect*, EUP, Edinburgh 1961, pp xi-xix.
10. Nairn, *The Break-up of Britain: Crisis and Neo-Nationalism*, New Left Books, London 1977, esp. Ch. 4; Harvie, *Scotland and Nationalism: Scottish Society and Politics 1707-1977*, Allen and Unwin, London 1977, Ch. 3.
11. A. Gramsci, 'The Intellectuals', in idem, *The Prison Notebooks*, Lawrence and Wishart, London 1971, p 18.
12. Harvie, op. cit., pp 125ff.
13. R. Watson, *The Literature of Scotland*, Schocken, London, New York 1986, pp 469-73.
14. E. Muir, *Scottish Journey*, Heinemann/Gollancz, London 1935, p 116.
15. T. Johnston, *Memories*, Collins, Glasgow 1952, p 33.
16. Scottish Secretariat Papers, National Library of Scotland, Edinburgh: R. E. Muirhead, 'Autobiographical Writings'.
17. R. B. Cunninghame-Graham, *Scottish Stories*, Cape, London 1914, esp. 'The Colonel' and 'A Braw Day'.
18. See S. Gwynn (ed), *The Anvil War*, Macmillan, London 1936, p 19; and J. Adam Smith, *John Buchan*, Hart Davis, London 1965, pp 153-4.
19. Hanham, op. cit., pp 42ff.
20. See the debates on the Government of Scotland Bill, 1913 and 1914, in *Hansard*, Vol. 53, Cols. 471-542, and Vol. 62, Cols. 1471-1543.
21. Carlyle, *Heroes and Hero-Worship*, 1840, Tauchnitz 1916, p 195.
22. See J. Gross, *The Rise and Fall of the Man of Letters: Aspects of English Literary Life Since 1900*, Penguin, Harmondsworth 1973 (London 1969), p 134.
23. W. Donaldson, *Popular Literature in Victorian Scotland*, AUP, Aberdeen 1986, pp ix-xii.
24. Ibid., pp 149-150.
25. T. W. H. Crosland, *The Unspeakable Scot*, Grant Richards, London 1900, Ch. 4.
26. Not completely. T. S. Law writes under the name of Thurso Berwick and Tom Nairn chose to appear as D. A. MacIver in *The Bulletin of Scottish Politics*, No. 1, 1980.

27. One has the distinct feeling that many of the assaults on MacDiarmid's *Contemporary Scottish Studies* in the *Scottish Educational Journal*, 1926-27, were the work of the author himself.
28. *Albyn or the Future of the Scots*, quoted in D. Glen, *Hugh MacDiarmid and the Scottish Renaissance*, Charles, Edinburgh, London 1964, p 48.
29. J. A. A. Porteous calculated that Scots war deaths were 8.7% higher in Scotland than in England: *Scotland and the South*, Scottish Covenant Movement, Edinburgh 1947, p 26.
30. A. K. Cairncross, 'New Industries and Economic Development in Scotland', in *Three Banks Review*, No. 7, 1952, p 5.
31. R. Campbell, *The Rise and Fall of Scottish Industry, 1707-1939*, John Donald, Edinburgh 1980, p 171.
32. Brand, op. cit., p 24.
33. Ibid., p 198.
34. Op. cit., pp 15-22.
35. Ibid., p 77.
36. A. J. P. Taylor, *Beaverbrook*, Hamish Hamilton, London 1972, p 215.
37. Grieve, op. cit., p 72.
38. C. T. Harvie, *No Gods and Precious Few Heroes: Scotland Since 1914*, Arnold, London 1981, rev. ed. 1987, p 132.
39. See A. Bold, *MacDiarmid: a Critical Biography*, Murray, London 1988, p 171.
40. J. Cameron, *Point of Departure*, Arthur Barker, London 1966, pp 36ff.
41. Leaders of Scottish property and business interests signed a collective letter against home rule, published on 15 November 1932. Significantly, it was carried in the London *Times*.
42. Brand, op. cit., p 214.
43. See Hanham, op. cit., p 153, and Brand, op. cit., p 207.
44. C. Mackenzie, *My Life and Times: Octave Six*, Chatto and Windus, London 1967, p 159.
45. Scottish Secretariat MSS: R. E. Muirhead to A. Donaldson, 6 June 1931.
46. R. Douglas, *History of the Liberal Party, 1895-1970*, Sidgwick and Jackson, London 1971, pp 228-235.
47. Bold, *MacDiarmid*, p 264; E. Muir, *Social Credit and the Labour Party*, Stanley Nott, 1935.
48. Bold, op. cit., pp 318-9; 323ff.
49. *Hansard*, Vol. 272, Cols. 261-267; Debate on the Address of 24 November 1932.
50. Quoted in *Scots Independent*, April 1936, p 4.
51. J. M. Reid, *James Lithgow: Master of Work*, Hutchison, London 1964, pp 146-156.
52. Sir C. Coote, *A Companion of Honour: the Story of Walter Elliot*, Collins, London 1965, pp 104ff.
53. Quoted in Brand, op. cit., p 101.
54. Cited in S. Maxwell, art. cit., p 219.
55. Maxwell, loc. cit.
56. E. Barnouw, *Documentary: A History of the Non-Fiction Film*, OUP, Oxford, pp 87ff.

57. Brand, op. cit., p 240.
58. Cf. C. T. Harvie, 'The Recovery of Scottish Labour, 1939-1951', in
    I. Donnachie, C. T. Harvie, I. S. Woods (eds), *Forward! Labour Politics
    in Scotland 1888-1988*, Polygon, Edinburgh 1989, pp 66ff.
59. MacDiarmid to Muirhead, 5 November 1928, in A. Bold, *The Letters
    of Hugh MacDiarmid*, Hamish Hamilton, London 1984, pp 296ff.

The Impact of 1979 on the SNP

1. Stephen Maxwell, SNP candidate for Edinburgh Pentlands quoted in
   The Scotsman, 5 May 1979.
2. James Callaghan, *Time and Chance*, 1987; also Bernard Donoghue,
   *Prime Minister: The Conduct of Policy Under Harold Wilson and
   James Callaghan*, 1987, as well as Denis Healey, *The Time of My Life*,
   1989.
3. As outlined in Gavin Kennedy (ed), *The Radical Approach*, 1976.
4. Gordon Brown, Introduction to *The Red Paper on Scotland*, 1975.
5. Full details in R. Parry (ed), *Scottish Political Facts*, 1988.
6. Jack Brand, *The National Movement in Scotland*, 1978, pp 283-87.
7. The ASNTU was disbanded by the NEC in 1980. However, a new SNP
   Trade Union Group was set up in 1984, as an affiliated body.
8. Ian Bayne, 'Can the West be Won?', *Q (Question)*, October 1975.
9. Arguably, the 1934 merger between the 'left-wing' National Party of
   Scotland, formed in 1928, and the 'right-wing' Scottish Party, founded
   in 1933, which established the SNP, was itself an implicit recognition
   that political nationalism in Scotland could only advance across a broad
   electoral front; and this remained a central element in the party's
   strategic approach to the electorate at least until the late 1970s. See also
   Brand, *The National Movement*, especially Ch. 12 and 13.
10. Brand, pp 63-64, 145-47.
11. Stephen Maxwell, 'Beyond Social Democracy', in G. Kennedy (ed), *The
    Radical Approach*.
12. James Mitchell, 'Recent developments and Underlying Trends in the
    SNP', unpublished paper delivered to the 1987 PSA conference.
13. Stephen Maxwell, *The Case For Left-Wing Nationalism*, 1981.
14. J. Bochel, D. Denver and A. Macartney (eds), *The Referendum
    Experience – Scotland 1979*, Aberdeen 1981, especially Ch. 8.
15. Stephen Maxwell, letter to *The Scotsman*, 4 December 1981; see also
    reply from Ian O. Bayne, *The Scotsman*, 11 December 1981, as well as
    initial letter from ex-SNP MP Douglas Crawford, *The Scotsman*,
    2 December 1981.
16. Another post-1979 fringe group, Siol nan Gaidheal (Seed of the Gael),
    had already caused the leadership considerable embarrassment due to
    its pseudo-Gaelic cultural pretensions as well as its neo-fascist and even
    racist undercurrents; a resolution effectively proscribing this organ-
    isation had been passed at the September 1981 meeting of the SNP
    National Council.

17. One of the 'magnificent seven' expellees, Kenny McAskill, even stood as the party's candidate for Livingston at the 1983 election – so much for the 'Fundamentalist' purge of the Left.

18. Ian O. Bayne, 'Opportunity for SNP but Tories face dilemmas', *Glasgow Herald*, 6 August 1987.

19. Ironically the most prominent convert to the SNP between general elections of 1983 and 1987 was ex-Tory candidate Iain Lawson, disgruntled at the closure of Gartcosh steel mill; he contested Stirling at the 1987 election against former colleague, Michael Forsyth.

20. A point underlined by the January 1990 resignation from the SNP of two Grampian regional councillors, including former SNP MP Hamish Watt, partly in protest against the poll-tax non-payment campaign.

21. A reference to an English professional pugilist recently thrashed in a world heavyweight championship title fight.

22. This verdict received ample confirmation in the 1990 Regional elections. The SNP failed to make any real impact on the Labour vote in urban-industrial areas and, despite good results in Grampian Region, it only made a net gain of three seats, together with an extra 3% of the vote, in Scotland as a whole.

23. Bill Miller, 'Can We Believe Opinion Polls?' in D. McCrone (ed), *What Scotland Wants: Ten Years On,* 1989.

24. But note that there was also a Scottish anti-Labour majority – albeit a much narrower one – at the 1987 election. See Ian O. Bayne, 'Independence Strategy', *Scots Independent,* August 1987.

25. J. MacCormick, *The Flag in the Wind,* 1955, p 198.

26. MacCormick, op. cit., p 109; a phrase used to characterise the cross-party pressure group, Scottish Convention, launched by MacCormick in 1942 when he led a breakaway group from the SNP and later responsible for convening a series of meetings of a representative Scottish National Assembly which in 1949 launched the Scottish Covenant, a declaration pledging its – ultimately two million – signatories 'to do everything in our power to secure for Scotland a Parliament with adequate legislative authority in Scottish affairs'.

The Lessons of Ireland

1. Quoted in Robert Blake, *Disraeli*, London 1966, p 179.

2. *Scotland's Welcome to Mr Parnell: Souvenir of His First Political Visit to Scotland,* Edinburgh 1889, p 72.

3. See T. W. Moody, *Davitt and Irish Revolution,* Oxford, 1981, p 125. Also Ian S. Wood, 'Irish Nationalism and Radical Politics in Scotland 1880-1906', in *The Journal of the Scottish Labour History Society,* No. 9, June 1975, pp 21-37, and 'Irish Immigrants and Scottish Radicalism', in Ian MacDougall (ed), *Essays in Scottish Labour History,* Edinburgh, 1978.

4. The readers of this journal voted Delia Larkin the woman who had contributed most to the nationalist movement, for her role during the 1913 Dublin strike and lock-out.
5. See Wendy Wood, *I Like Life,* Edinburgh and London, 1938.
6. Quoted in Sir Reginald Coupland, *Welsh and Scottish Nationalism, a study,* London, 1954, p 398.
7. MacCormick, Dr John, *The Flag in the Wind,* London, 1955, p 67.
8. Ibid., pp 83-4.
9. John Hutchinson, *The Dynamics of Cultural Nationalism,* London, 1987, p 152.
10. Ibid., p 153.
11. James Plunkett, *The Trusting and the Maimed,* London, 1959, pp 83-84.
12. Document in writer's possession.
13. Owen Dudley Edwards, 'Ireland', in Edward, Evans, Rhys and MacDiarmid, *Celtic Nationalism,* London, 1968, p 89.
14. This was epitomised in Thomas Johnston's books *Our Noble Families* and *The History of the Working Classes in Scotland.* The latter was inspired by Connolly's *Labour in Irish History* and paralleled its exposure of suffering and exploitation on the one hand and privilege and perfidy on the other. It also perpetuated the myth of Celtic Communism and suggested that the modern socialist movement was reviving the co-operation and mutual aid which had been eradicated by feudalism. This drew on a tradition which was common to all the nations of these islands. In England it is known as the 'myth of the Norman Yoke', but it had a different resonance in Ireland and Scotland. In England it meant that the people had once been free and that radicalism was struggling against an internal enemy – the wealthy and powerful – to regain their original state of liberty. In Ireland it meant that too; but the enemy was seen as an external one and freedom was to be won through political independence. In Scotland it referred to both an internal and an external enemy. In both Scotland and England it could be associated with the Glorious Revolution and the struggle against Stuart absolutism, a linkage which was impossible for Irish nationalism.
15. Quoted in John Bowman, *De Valera and the Ulster Question,* Oxford, 1982, p 275. For a discussion of the Anti-Partition League see Bob Purdie, 'The Irish Anti-Partition League, South Armagh and the Abstentionist Tactic 1948-58', *Irish Political Studies 1,* 1986, pp 67-77.
16. John Bowman records that the Mansion House Committee referred to Unionist voters as 'Quisling Irish', op. cit. p 273.
17. The insularity of many Irish nationalists of the time was epitomised by the speech made at an Anti-Partition rally in Crossmaglen in 1946, when partition was denounced as, 'the greatest crime ever to be perpetrated against any country in the world'. See *Irish News,* 21 January 1946.
18. See the autobiography of former IRA Chief of Staff Séan Mac Stíofáin, *Memoirs of a Revolutionary,* Edinburgh, 1975, pp 34-7, for an account of this involvement with and disillusion in the Anti-Partition Campaign.

19. *Guardian,* 16 March 1990.
20. H. C. Deb. 736: 225 15 November 1966.
21. J. P. Mackintosh, *The Devolution of Power, Local Democracy, Regionalism and Nationalism,* Harmondsworth, 1968, p 173.
22. Martin Wallace, 'Home Rule in Northern Ireland – Anomalies of Devolution', *Northern Ireland Legal Quarterly,* Vol. 18, No. 1, June 1967, p 161.
23. John C. Duffy, 'A Reviving Proposal. The Powers That Be. Should the Northern Ireland Government Have More Powers?', *New Ireland,* Vol. 1, No. 1, 1963, pp 26-7.
24. History was repeating itself. In 1950 Oliver Brown stood in Greenock as a joint Scottish Nationalist-Irish Anti-Partitionist candidate, but gleaned only 718 votes, a percentage of 1.8. (The Communist candidate, in this chilly period of the Cold War, got nearly 3.0%.)
25. *The Scotsman,* 13 May 1987.
26. Ibid., 7 May 1987.
27. Seamus Heaney, 'Whatever You Say Say Nothing', in *North,* London, 1975.
28. Rosemary Harris, *Prejudice and Tolerance in Ulster,* Manchester, 1972, pp 143-4.
29. *Irish Weekly,* 15 January 1966.
30. Richard Rose, *Governing Without Consensus: an Irish Perspective,* London, 1971, pp 479 and 481-2.
31. Owen Dudley Edwards, 'Wales, Scotland and Ireland', in John Osmond (ed), *The National Question Again,* Dyfed Llandysul, 1985, p 51.
32. See the writer's *Politics in the Streets. The Origins of the Civil Rights Movement in Northern Ireland,* Belfast, 1990.

The SNP and the Lure of Europe

1. Robert Lane, *The Scotsman,* 21 March 1989.
2. *The Scotsman,* 9 June 1989.
3. Ibid.
4. *Glasgow Herald,* 14 April 1989.
5. Bryan Gould, *New European,* Summer 1988.
6. J. K. Galbraith, *The New Industrial State,* 1974.
7. Standing Commission on the Scottish Economy, Final Report, 1989.
8. Neal Ascherson, *Observer,* 1 October 1989.
9. Allan Macartney, *Radical Scotland,* Dec./Jan. 1990.
10. Ewen MacAskill, *Scotsman,* 7 October 1989.
11. E. H. Carr, *Nationalism and After,* 1945.

The SNP and the Scottish Working Class

1. J. Cornford and J. Brand, 'Scottish Voting Behaviour', in J. N. Wolfe (ed), *Government and Nationalism in Scotland*, Aberdeen University Press, 1969.
2. M. Fry, *Patronage and Principle*, Aberdeen University Press, 1987, p 227.
3. T. Gallagher, *Glasgow, The Uneasy Place*, Manchester University Press, 1987, see Ch. 7.
4. Cornford and Brand, 'Scottish Voting Behaviour'.
5. C. Harvie, *Scotland and Nationalism*, Allen and Unwin, 1977, p 148.
6. The conference addresses of the major party leaders are usually broadcast live.
7. *The Scotsman*, 25 September 1989.
8. *Observer Scotland*, 9 October 1988.
9. Harvie, *Scotland and Nationalism*, p 264.
10. C. Harvie, *No Gods and Precious Few Heroes, Scotland Since 1914*, Edward Arnold, 1981, p 162.
11. See H. Drucker, *Breakaway*, Polygon, 1977.
12. J. Brand et al, 'National Consciousness and Voting in Scotland', paper presented at the conference of the Political Science Association, Hull, 1981, pp 15-6.
13. Brand et al, p 15.
14. M. Keating, *Glasgow, The City That Refused To Die*, Aberdeen University Press, 1988, p 57.
15. Interview given by the author about the book mentioned in note 14, the *Evening Times*, Glasgow, 1 December 1988.
16. C. Harvie, in K. Cargill (ed), *Scotland 2000*, BBC Publications, Glasgow, p 31.
17. *Scotland On Sunday*, 5 November 1989.
18. Information from Govan SNP member.
19. *New Statesman and Society*, 28 October 1988.
20. See note 17.
21. The speeches by MPs Margaret Ewing and Alex Salmond strongly conveyed this attitude. The fullest account of the National Council meeting appeared in the *Glasgow Herald*, 13 February 1989.
22. *Glasgow Herald*, 22 September 1989.
23. Interview with SNP activist.
24. D. Douglas, 'Profile of Kenny McAskill', *Glasgow Herald*, 28 May 1990.
25. Jim Sillars, *Scotland On Sunday*, 1 July 1989.
26. Address given at the Young Students Nationalist conference, 10 March 1989.
27. R. Graham, *Spain, Change of a Nation*, London, 1984, p 185.
28. Cargill, *Scotland 2000*, p 11.
29. Gordon Wilson, Young Student Nationalist conference, March 1989.
30. See note 26.
31. Speech at the opening of the Constitutional Convention, 30 March 1989.

32. According to Ruth Wishart in the *The Scotsman*, 29 March 1989.
33. Quoted in the *Independent*, 23 September 1989.
34. Alex Salmond, Young Student Nationalists conference in Edinburgh, November 1989.
35. Sentiments publicly expressed by two party members at Young Student Nationalists conference in Edinburgh, 10 November 1989.
36. Isobel Lindsay, 6th meeting of the Constitutional Convention, 27 September 1990.

The Scottish Middle Class and the National Debate

1. C. Moore and S. Booth, *Managing Competition: Meso-corporatism Pluralism and the Negotiated Order in Scotland*, OUP, 1989.
2. J. Bochel, D. Denver and A. Macartney, *The Referendum Experience*, Aberdeen University Press, 1981, p 142.
3. S. Kendrick, F. Bechhofer, D. McCrone, 'Is Scotland Different? Industrial and Occupational Change in Scotland and Britain', in Newby et al (eds), *Restructuring Capital*, Macmillan, 1985.
4. S. Kendrick, 'Occupational Change in Modern Scotland', in D. McCrone (ed), *Scottish Government Yearbook 1986*, Edinburgh.
5. S. Maxwell, 'The Treason of the Clerks', in *Scottish International Review*, September and October 1972, Vol. 5, Nos. 6, 7, Edinburgh.
6. R. Rose, *Class Equals Party: The Decline of a Model of British Voting*, Centre for the Study of Public Policy, University of Strathclyde, Glasgow, 1980.
7. R. Rose, op. cit.
8. R. Rose, op. cit.
9. J. Foster, *Scotland's Economy: Claiming the Future*, Scottish Trades Union Congress, Glasgow, 1989, p 13.
10. D. Butler and D. Kavanagh, *The British General Election 1987*, London, 1988, p 162.
11. R. Johnston, C. Pattie and T. Allsopp, *A Nation Dividing: the Electoral Map of Great Britain in 1979-1987*, London, 1988, p 142.
12. *Final Report*, Standing Commission on the Scottish Economy, November 1989, Glasgow.
13. *A Claim of Right for Scotland*, Scottish Constitutional Convention, Edinburgh, 1988.
14. A. Balfour, *Scottish Business Insider*, August 1989, Vol. 6, No. 8.
15. D. McCrone, 'Scottish Opinion Polls', in *The Scottish Government Yearbook 1989*, A. Brown and D. McCrone (eds), Edinburgh, 1989.
16. Ch. 2 Standing Commission on the Scottish Economy, op cit.
17. J. P. Mackintosh, *A Parliament for Scotland*, East Lothian Constituency Labour Party, 1976; and 'The Trouble with Stephen Maxwell', in H. Drucker (ed), *J. P. Mackintosh on Scotland*, Longman, 1982.

Conclusion

1. *Sunday Time,* 28 April 1991.
2. *The Observer,* 24 March 1991.
3. *The Observer,* 24 March 1991.
4. *Scots Independent,* January 1991.
5. *Radical Scotland,* No. 50, April-May 1991.
6. *Radical Scotland,* No. 49, February-March 1991.
7. *The Scotsman,* 26 February 1991.

11

Notes on Contributors

Ian O. Bayne Teacher in further education and a vigorous contributor to the Scottish press on educational topics and the political scene in Scotland. He is a long-standing member of the SNP and has fought three parliamentary contests for the party. He is secretary of the 1820 Society which exists to honour the memory of the Scottish radical weavers executed following the abortive rising of that year.

Tom Gallagher Reader in Peace Studies, University of Bradford; member of the Labour Party; author of *Portugal* (a study of its twentieth-century politics and history); *Glasgow: The Uneasy Peace* (on ethnic relations, rivalry and conflict).

Christopher Harvie Professor of British and Irish Studies, University of Tubingen. Member of the SNP and associate of the Scottish Council for Economic and Social Research. Author of *The Lights of Liberalism: University Liberals and the Challenge of Democracy 1860-86; Scotland and Nationalism: Scottish Society and Politics 1707-1977; No Gods and Precious Few Heroes: Scotland Since 1914-1980;* and *The Centre of Things: Political Fiction from Disraeli to the Present.*

Isobel Lindsay Lecturer in Sociology, University of Strathclyde; author of papers and reports on Scotland's demography and the structure of its society. Member of the SNP, former parliamentary candidate and member of the National Executive. Convener of the Campaign for a Scottish Assembly since 1990.

Stephen Maxwell Senior Policy Analyst, Scottish Council of Voluntary Organisations. Author of a study of multi-nationalist capitalist organisations with particular reference to Scotland. Member of the SNP and former parliamentary candidate and elected representative as well as senior party office-bearer.

Bob Purdie Tutor in Politics, Ruskin College, Oxford. *Politics In The Streets,* his study of the Northern Ireland Civil Rights Movement, was published in 1990. Joined the SNP in 1988 following a number of years spent in Northern Ireland as a researcher and political activist, latterly concerned with achieving common ground among adherents of the unionist and nationalist traditions by emphasising issues of common importance to them.